"*Everything you find inside is* handmade without preservatives or any other nasties"

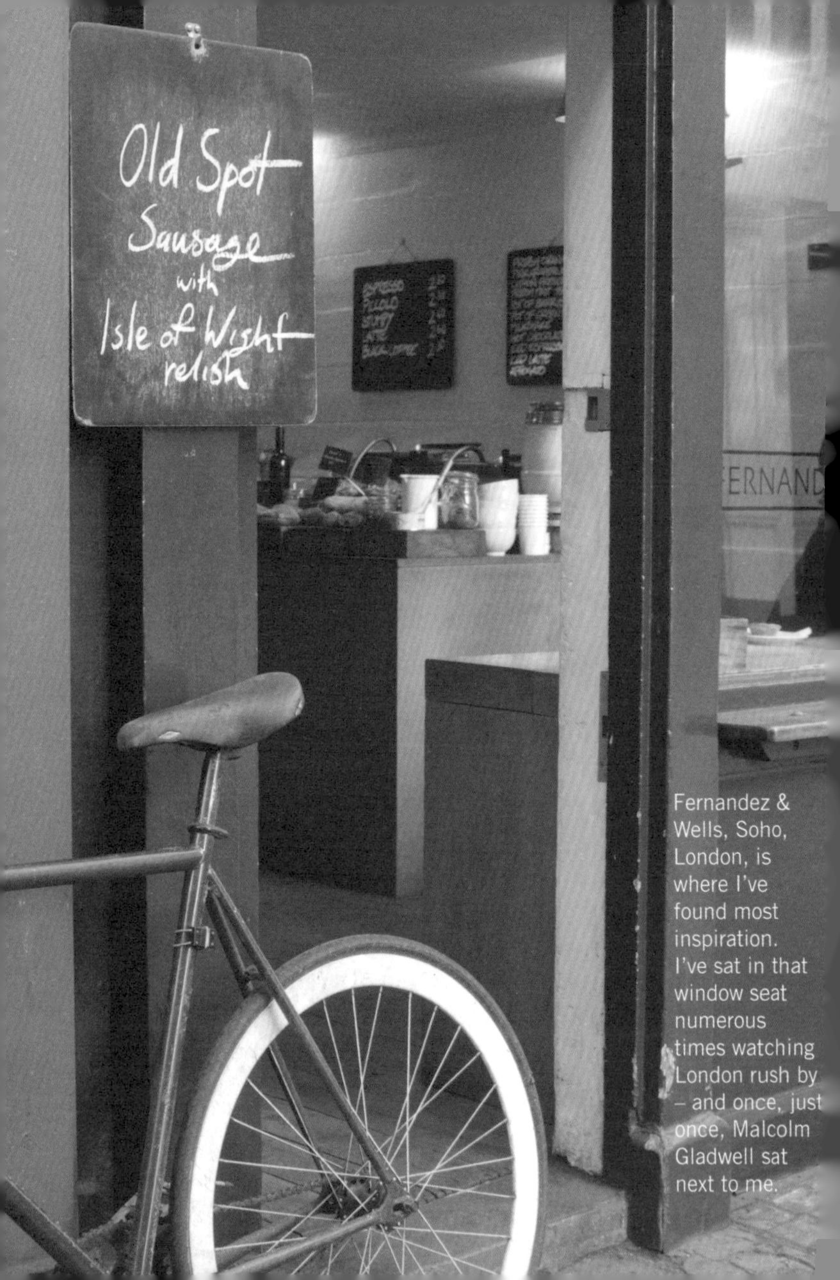
Old Spot Sausage
with
Isle of Wight relish
FERNAND

Fernandez & Wells, Soho, London, is where I've found most inspiration. I've sat in that window seat numerous times watching London rush by – and once, just once, Malcolm Gladwell sat next to me.

1   Kick-ass coffee
    Powering great ideas since 1680

2   Nine-2-Five reasons
    To work fewer office hours

3   Change your life
    Work where you like

4   Change the world around you
    Success stories from 'Out of Office'

5   Which hot spot will it be today?
    The whole of life in every day

6   Penny University
    Crucial life lessons from today's smartest thinkers

7   Build your network
    The six people you need

8   Be the best team player
    Ten tips for maintaining great working relationships

9   Create the best ideas
    With the help of everyone around you

10 Maximise sales
    By helping everyone around you

11 Join the 'Work Where You Like' movement

The excellent Prufrock Coffee in Clerkenwell, East London. Free Wi-Fi at the home of World Champion barista Gwilym Davies and a place where baristas learn to serve the coffee that powers you and your ideas.

Hi,

Thanks for opening the book. It is a labour of love. Working 'Out of Office' is a way of life I totally believe in and so I wanted to make sure I captured everything that will help anyone get the most out of it.

I always struggled to get the best from myself working full-time under one roof, struggling with the silence and the politics and thinking there must be more to life than this. We moved into central London and a new coffee shop opened opposite from that day forward I found a new way of life...

Rather than putting the rat race first, I found a permanent 'Out of Office' state of mind; of freedom, inspiration and vibrancy. It enables me to be more productive and creative but to also enjoy living life to the full.

As free Wi-Fi spreads I see the number of people around me with laptops, tablets and smartphones grow enormously. All enjoying being busy, creative and relaxed. It's great to see.

This book is a result of being asked so many times how to do it. How to live life to the full, work where you like, when you like and still produce the most effective work.

The answers are all here.
Please let me know what you think and share your own stories.

chris@workwhereyoulike.com

" The 'Last Exit On Brooklyn' coffee house was one of Seattle's great `60s landmarks, a gathering place for students, radicals, poets, nut jobs, chess masters, teens, intellectuals, workers, musicians, artists, beatniks, and hippies.

I remember the din, the open-mike music, cigarette smoke, impromptu poetry readings, the arguments of lefties, libertarians, crackpots, and cultists.

You could hear the rhythm and roar of the counterculture as it lived and breathed."

Seattle writer and journalist Knute Berger on The Last Exit On Brooklyn coffee house.

Kick-ass coffee
Powering great ideas since 1680

For more than 300 years, expert baristas have served the finest espresso to people like you – the music makers, storytellers, poets, legends, entrepreneurs, activists, champions and digital pioneers, those with vision and dreamers of dreams.

The enlivening properties of caffeine and the community of the coffee shop have been behind many of history's revolutions and movements in politics, music, art, storytelling and business. Inspired customers, innovating and sharing ideas, are the people who have changed the world.

It started 500 years ago with political gatherings of Imams in the coffee houses of Mecca.

In 1689, Edward Lloyd founded one of the most successful businesses of all time, Lloyds of London, from his own coffee shop. Over strong espressos, Isaac Newton, Christopher Wren and the philosopher Robert Hooke met to discuss the movement of the Earth, and Dr John Wilkins dared share his dream that man could one day fly to the moon.

On the West Coast of the US in the nineteenth and twentieth centuries, writers, poets, musicians and artists congregated in laid-back coffee houses to share their music and ideas, culminating in the political folk movement led by Bob Dylan and Joan Baez in the 1960s.

During the 1930s, the famous neighbouring Parisian cafes, Les Deux Magots and Café de Flore, hosted long heated debates featuring the greatest intellectuals and artists of the day, including Ernest Hemingway, Albert Camus, Pablo Picasso and Jean-Paul Satre.

The political messages of the French and Russian revolutions, the fall of the Berlin Wall and the Arab Spring were all hatched far from the authorities' office blocks in backstreet coffee houses. Word spread around the tables, inspiring the people to stand up and change their own lives and the world around them.

From 1967, the Last Exit On Brooklyn coffee house in Seattle was the home to counterculture. Three residents, Jerry, Zev and Gordon loved it and started their own shop called Starbucks.. and coffee shop culture began to spread across the world.

Yet some of that culture disappeared from the 1980s when we burdened ourselves with technology that we couldn't afford on our own and wouldn't fit in our bags. Photocopiers, fax machines and telephone systems drew us into office blocks where we were confined, apart from the few internet cafes that opened up to serve those who found working in an office, alone at home or in a studio, unbearable.

Listening to Dylan at the classic Paris cafe, Verlet

In 2002, a third wave of the coffee movement transformed the market, led by the likes of coffee roasters Stumptown and Intelligentsia in the US, St. Ali in Australia and Allpress Espresso and Atomic Coffee Roasters in New Zealand. The highest quality coffee beans are now treated as artisan products, like the very best wine or chocolate. Single origin coffee is topped with latte art. Your coffee comes served with the utmost passion and authenticity.

By around 2005, the size and cost of office machines had been reduced to more powerful mobile versions that could fit in our pockets. More importantly, widely available Wi-Fi and the growing number of coffee shops, enabled us to untie ourselves from the desk and work wherever we wanted.

In the digital age, the 'Out of Office' movement is growing faster than ever, fuelled by entrepreneurs, artists and flexitime workers, on their mobiles, tablets and laptops in what some refer to as their 'coffices'. We are also seeing the fast expansion of co-working hubs providing start-ups with office support, amid a similar atmosphere to a coffee shop.

The $100million sales of Moshi Monsters began over a macchiato in London. Craig Newmark started his craigslist website in a coffee shop on the US West Coast. The 50 million check-ins of Foursquare were inspired and built in two New York coffee shops. Barack Obama's first inauguration speech was written in a Starbucks and Harry Potter, the most successful fictional character of all time, was born in a small Edinburgh café.

Out of Office re: book final draft

chris ward to me

Hi, I'm up against the deadline to finish my book and so I'm with an espresso in a good coffee shop, maximising inspiration and productivity.

If your enquiry is urgent, please contact the brilliant helen@bluedotworld.com

Thanks.

Chris

----
uk.linkedin.com/in/chrisatcoffice

twitter.com/chrisatcoffice

Red Nose Day 09   1GOAL World Cup 2010
Mandela Day 2013 LDN Olympics 2012

Are you going to share pictures of cats or change the world?

Today, you can achieve far more than you have ever previously been able to when tied to your desk.

You can be left to your own (mobile) devices and measured on your productivity, not your presence.

You can achieve your work in far less than the 40 hours considered necessary to complete every job, in every role, in every office block, in every country in the world.

Being in an office for 40 hours, but completing work in less time, means people are seeking inspiration elsewhere, sharing more and more pictures of cats and sending more and more emails, all to someone sitting a couple of feet away from them.

'Out of Office', you are inspired by what's around you. Your inspiration is people, the very same people who respond, engage, buy, read, listen, wear or play with the ideas you are creating. The same people who inspire you to come up with the best ideas, songs, books, movies, design or artwork. The same people who can become your biggest fans or customers.

The very people whose lives you can change, sit next to you.

I did it so can you

All the benefits of working flexibly and remotely has enabled me to go from schoolboy failure to starting and selling two successful businesses and helping raise hundreds of millions of pounds for charity. The campaigns I produce now are more creative and successful than when I worked 12 hours a day in the same office.

The time saved by maximising my productivity also enables me to spend as much time as I want with my wife and four children, as well as cycle and run marathons around the world.

I love to work somewhere cool, on a nice big communal table with my laptop, espresso, a glass of tap water and something made from chocolate!

This gets me into a positive and productive flow that can last for hours, meaning I get home relaxed and satisfied that I have genuinely achieved what I set out to do that day.

This 'Out of Office' manifesto is my life, together with other people's inspiring stories of success and a step-by-step guide to achieving it yourself.

You don't have to settle for just climbing the corporate ladder. Wake up – smell the coffee! Join Picasso, Dylan, J.K. Rowling, Richard Branson and many others. Ask for the Wi-Fi password and change your life and the world around you.

HERE STOOD
THE FIRST LONDON
COFFEE HOUSE
AT THE SIGN OF
PASQUA ROSEE'S HEAD
1652

Some people go to Bethlehem, some to Mecca. I made my way on a cold night, to pay respects to the birthplace of coffee in the UK.

Not only do home workers reduce
the need for ~~~

Rupert Murdoch says fat cat
bosses are out of date, out of
touch and too big to change
direction.

Often that's because their
employees are busy sharing
pictures of cats.

the grou...
in cafés between
Seventy years ea...
Marx sketched
tracts in other
Paris. The Fr...
working-cla...
full circle, t...
communi...
closed do...

Rupert Murdoch gave a talk recently in which he explained the game-changing effect of the digital age on his industry. For the media baron, the story of website The Drudge Report says it all. As many know, American Matt Drudge built a global readership by aggregating mainly conservative articles and links on his site, the popularity and notoriety of which skyrocketed when he broke the Monica Lewinsky scandal.

As Murdoch explained, Drudge accomplished all this without renting office space, hiring a large staff, investing a king's ransom in technology or even bothering to take out an ad – all the things a budding media tycoon would have had to do a few short years ago to get such an enterprise off the ground. He did it all from his apartment and a local café in Miami Beach, Florida, with nothing more than a computer and broadband link, a nose for news and a good idea.

Far from lamenting this revolution, the tycoon sounded quite wistful about it. Imagine how much easier and cheaper it would be to build a global media emp... today. Anyway, you have to ask, who ...k at a desk when you can do ...

Stron...

One ...
Euro...
one...
– ...
sa...
a...

Rory, a top advertising guru, says that the great author Nassim Taleb concluded there's a scientific reason the coffee shop is the best place to be productive

> *"In his book Antifragile, Nassim Nicholas Taleb explains why he works in cafés in terms of 'Stochastic Resonance' – the idea that a weak signal becomes easier to detect if you add white noise in the background. The reasoning is that it is easier to maintain a train of thought in the presence of a certain amount of random background activity.*
> *In a café you are never actually disturbed, unless someone briefly asks, "Is this seat free?" But at the same time you do not have to struggle against a background of silence."*

Rory Sutherland, Executive Creative Director and Vice-Chairman, OgilvyOne London and Vice-Chairman, Ogilvy & Mather UK

Michael, who has sold $100million worth of Moshi Monsters, says it's the best place to be creative

> *"I like working out of coffee shops because you can work deeply without getting disturbed but if you need a jolt of visual stimulus you can look up and there'll be endless things to inspire you."*

Michael Acton Smith, CEO, Creative Director and founder of Moshi Monsters

It says here you can be 20% more productive in 50% less time

Is your boss measuring you on your productivity or your presence?

"*Bosses who continue to insist that people go to work at the same time and stick to a set routine may actually weaken morale and business performance. People don't generally like being told how to run their life. They feel their boss is controlling them and therefore are actually less motivated. By contrast bosses who equip staff with technological means to work flexibly and remotely, reap the benefits of a more committed, goal-orientated workforce.*"

Graham Jones, Internet Psychologist

The office is being made redundant

Expensive
Infrastructure
40 Hours
Office Hours
Assistants
Desktop
Headache tablet
Corner office
Research
Cloudy weather
Company ID
Overtime
Bank loan
Routine

You can do everything you want from anywhere you like

Economical
Apps
20 hours
Opening hours
Smart phones
Laptop
Handheld tablet
Window seat
Experience
Cloud storage
Community
Time gentleman, please
Crowdsource
Flexibility

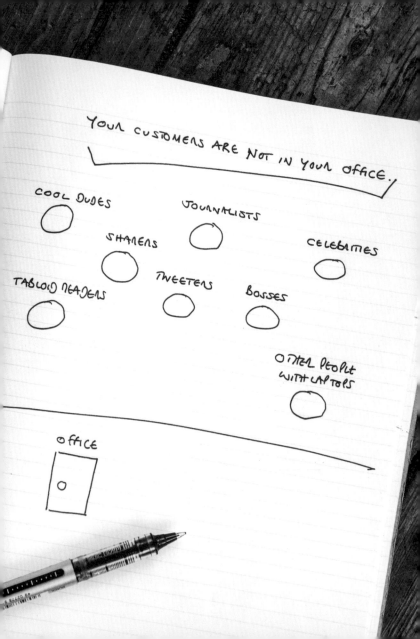

> *"It's very easy to think that you are the expert on your own product. The true experts are your customers."*

Jamie Wong, CEO, Vayable

> *"You can have all the focus groups in the world but unless you're mixing with normal people, how do you know what different kinds of people will think?"*

Sadiq Khan, Shadow Minister for London

> *"The wisest decisions are made by those closest to the problem, regardless of their seniority."*

Stanley McChrystal, Ret. General US Army

Work next to customers who have problems

The most successful new ideas are those that answer a problem. "There's no book for this subject I want to read about." "There's no product that will do what I want." "There's no one offering the service I need."

The more people who have the same problem, the bigger the opportunity!

Everyone has customers – clients or the public. All your 'customers' hang out in coffee shops. Solve their problems and you will have created your new business.

In offices the answer is often searched for through research.

You never need to research anything again.

You get to really know what customers' problems are by working right next to them.

Work next to customers who can solve them

Comic Relief founder Richard Curtis told me that he used to write his TV comedies in a quiet BBC office. He didn't know which were the funny lines, until he could hear someone coming up the stairs towards him. He then instantly knew which were the best jokes by anticipating that persons' reaction to the punch line.

When you are surrounded by 'customers' you get a good sense of whether they will like the idea that is forming in your head or not. That will not happen in a silent office or if you are only surrounded by people who are trying to solve the same problem as you.

You need the inspiration and input of the most relevant 'customers' and you won't find them in your office. The best global experts in your field and your future customers are sitting in coffee shops.

Hang out in the ones that can give you the answer. Mix what you pick up with the thoughts of the most relevant customers in coffee shops anywhere in the world, through blogs, Twitter and Facebook.

STORE STRE

NOW

At the opening of another great London coffee shop.

Don't spend life climbing a ladder

Retire	**65**	
Gold watch	**60**	
CEO	**50**	Cycle Tour de France route
	49	Run Mandela Day campaign
	48	Founded social currency
	47	Social legacy 2012 Olympics
	46	Legacy of the 2010 World Cup
	44	Creative Director, Comic Relief
	43	Worked in African orphanage
Director	**42**	Hardest mountain bike races
	41	Founded sports social network
	40	Ran ten international marathons
Vice President	**38**	Sold two agencies
	37	PR Campaign of the Year award
	33	Fastest-growing PR agency
Senior Exec	**32**	
	31	Married / four children
	30	Founded comms agency
Junior executive	**26**	
Trainee	**23**	Band manager
	19	BBC record library assistant
	17	Chemist shop assistant
Work experience	**16**	Art student
	15	Left school - 1 qualification

Just enjoy it...

People used to look up the ladder to company lifers, the people who reached the top, as the winners of the rat race they should aim to emulate.

But business leaders now reach their peak by 45 and then plateau, while feeling increasingly jealous of younger colleagues who are still climbing the ladder towards them.

They finished their rat race at 45 and are running on the spot.

They didn't have the drive or bravery to take the alternative route, a full and varied journey that lasts a lifetime.

That's not you, is it?

From top left: PR Week feature; all six of us running in Amsterdam; in Ethiopia with Comic Relief; finishing a ride across the French Pyrenees.

Don't be trapped in a rat race mentality

Unmotivated
Thinking done for you
Looking for a job
Clock watching
Motivated by pay
Show your face
Work in silence
Stress-fuelled bad mood
Gossip
Blame
Rewarded

I took this on my iPhone as I cycled passed. He looked lonely.

Be 'Out of Office' to live a full life

Mike Mathieson took a **photo** –
at Les Contamines – Montjoie
Today's office.

Self motivated
Thinking for yourself
Creating a job
Work when you feel like it
Motivated by great ideas
Show your work
Work in a hubbub
Brunch-fuelled good mood
Share
Responsibility
Rewarding

Mike runs one of the UK's most creative agencies, Cake. Before Wi-Fi
was invented we actually shared an office together!

Don't be a follower

In every office block, in every town, in every country, everyone typically works between 9am and 5pm, for five days of every single week. Everyone, it seems, takes five eight-hour days to get their job done.

That's too big a coincidence to be true, surely?

Our heroes, the people we follow are rarely in offices. So why are we?

Are you a follower or followed?

> *"We need to be working side-by-side. That is why it is critical that we are all present in our offices."*

Yahoo management memo to staff that created debate.

Be followed

"To successfully work with other people, you have to trust each other. A big part of this is trusting people to get their work done wherever they are, without supervision. It is the art of delegation, which has served Virgin and many other companies well over the years. We like to give people the freedom to work where they want, safe in the knowledge that they have the drive and expertise to perform excellently, whether they are at their desk or in their kitchen.

Yours truly has never worked out of an office, and never will.

We are in an age when remote working is easier and more effective than ever. If you provide the right technology to keep in touch, maintain regular communication and get the right balance between remote and office working, people will be motivated to work responsibly, quickly and with high quality.

Working life isn't nine to five any more. The world is connected. Companies that do not embrace this are missing a trick."

Richard Branson, Founder Virgin Group

Don't be desk bound

Want to make this a less regular sight?

Be outward bound

A favourite sight of mine, while working from the great Urban Reef cafe, right on the beach at Boscombe on the English south coast.

Don't be full-fat and poor

One of many great T-shirts from Howies Clothing says it all.

Be non-fat and rich

THIS ONE RUNS ON FAT AND SAVES YOU MONEY

Don't be treated like a child

**Are you TEMPTED
To leave your cup or mug here
and <u>wash it up</u> later????**

THINK AGAIN FRIENDS!

Please wash it up ASAP

Really need a reminder to do the basics?
Apparently the British Prime Minister
does, as I saw this on the bathroom door
at 10 Downing Street.

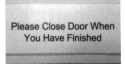

Please Close Door When
You Have Finished

Be treated like an adult

All the facilities you could ever need, at the best café for cyclists, look mum no hands!, Clerkenwell, London.

Don't drink bad coffee

Enjoy the very best coffee in the world

Stumptown

Toby's Estate

Third Rail

Cafe Grumpy

One afternoon in New York, just before our flight home, I decided to run round the city to try the four best espressos. I ended up flying, but only on caffeine – we managed to miss our flight.

Don't be stressed

Be desserts

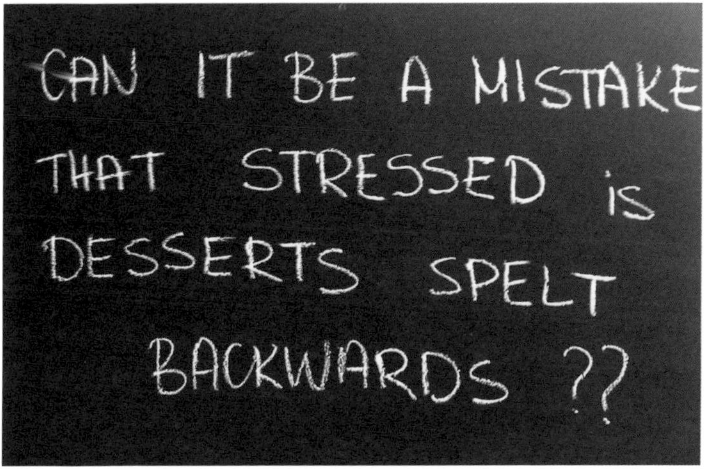

CAN IT BE A MISTAKE
THAT STRESSED is
DESSERTS SPELT
BACKWARDS ??

Don't pay per square foot

Just for a moment I'm going to step the other side of the counter and say a word on behalf of the coffee shops we work out of because they are too polite and nice to say it themselves.

They can only afford their rent based on the calories and caffeine you consume. They have a small problem: a few people who are working with their laptops only have one coffee, and they make it last for hours. We can't let that problem get any bigger if it leads to the coffee shop not being able to afford its rent.

Pay per calorie

In a coffee shop you will most likely spend more on food and drink than in an office, but you can choose to eat the very best, healthiest food – and it's still cheaper than leasing any office space.

This is the best brunch I've ever tasted, at Tasha's in Johannesburg, South Africa.

Don't be contracted

Be considerate

More in hope than expectation, I continue to give as much as I can to the Hummingbird Café in West London.

Don't be distracted and controlled

Many bosses control their employees.

Do you have any say about when your boss will appear over your shoulder, or any choice on what subject they'd like to interrupt you with?

Do you have control on where, when and what you work on?

Be distracted but free

Many young children in cafés can control their parents – but they haven't quite figured out how to control you yet.

It's easy to escape unwanted distractions by putting on some headphones or moving to another space.

You have control on where, when and what you work on.

Don't commute

Buy the cheapest bike to cycle around town and carry everything you can.

You want to make sure you have anything you might need for the day's work and the extra weight is perfect for turning those short rides into some good exercise.

I ride my wife's very cheap bike around town. With it being the wrong size and wrong weight (way too heavy!) it affords me some good exercise even though I'm only cycling five miles.

Exercise

Buy the best bike to race on.

Bike racing is one of the many new activities you can consider with all the extra time and fitness levels you gain.

What else could you now do? Marathon running? Charity trekking? Spend more time playing with family and friends?

I race on a great bike, built to fit and light. Perfect for cycling 200 miles on! This was at the end of a very long Gran Fondo race in the Italian Dolomites.

Don't give up

Most new ideas end in failure. If everyone was successful the word 'entrepreneur' wouldn't exist.

The Angry Birds mobile game is a global success for its producer Rovio but followed 51 other games that had failed for them.

Without the expense and infrastructure of an office you don't have to limit yourself to a once-in-a-lifetime go at launching ideas.

Without all those office leasing and commuting costs you are saving a fortune. The cost of using a coffee shop or hub is minimal in comparison. You can afford to try again, fail again and fail better.

Until you succeed.

The 99% perspiration and 1% inspiration you need can be achieved at Flatplanet, Soho, London. John Wooden was a basketball coach who originally said many of the quotes that still inspire today.

PERSISTENCE IS STRONGER THAN FAILURE.

From The Wisdom of John Wooden
Abraham Lincoln is acknowledged as one of America's greatest presidents.

Here is a brief summary of his career:

Failed in business: 1831

Defeated for legislature: 1832

Failed in business again: 1833

Elected to legislature: 1834

Sweetheart died: 1835

Had nervous breakdown: 1836

Defeated for speaker: 1836

Defeated for elector: 1840

Defeated for congressional nomination: 1843

Elected to Congress: 1846

Defeated for Congress: 1848

Defeated for Senate: 1855

Defeated for Vice President: 1856

Defeated for Senate: 1859

Elected President of the U.S.: 1860

The model Mr. Lincoln gave us with his persistence is
one we can remember in the face of our own setbacks.
And what is most wondrous of all is that persistence
is a quality that we ourselves control.

You, and only you, can decide whether you will stay the course.

(4) Change the world around you
Success stories from 'Out of Office'

SQUARE MILE
COFFEE·ROASTERS

"Obama inauguration:
Words of history crafted by
27-year-old in Starbucks"

Guardian newspaper headline 20th Jan 2009 about Jon Favreau,
Barack Obama's speech writer for his first inauguration speech,
delivered that same day.

J.K. Rowling, mother, author of Harry Potter

"The best place to write, in my opinion, is a café."

Over 450 million copies of the seven Harry Potter books have been sold worldwide and the eight movies grossed over $7.7billion.

"You don't feel that you are in solitary confinement while you work, and when inspiration fails, you can take a walk to the next cafe while your batteries recharge.

The best writing cafe is just crowded enough so that you blend in, but not so crowded that you end up sharing a table with somebody who tries to read chapter 20 upside down, has staff who don't glower at you if you sit there too long (though these days I can afford to keep ordering coffees even if I don't drink them, so that's less of a problem) and doesn't play very loud music, which is the only noise that disturbs me when I'm writing."

It was in Nicholson's Café and the Elephant House in Edinburgh where, as a hard-up single mother, J.K. Rowling famously penned her first Harry Potter novel.

Richard Tait, creator of Cranium

"That one cup of coffee led to us selling millions of games."

Cranium games sell in 20 countries and became the fastest-selling
independent board game in history. Richard is outside the original Pike
Place Starbucks in Seattle.

"I left Microsoft, and with partner Whit Alexander created a new board game called Cranium. We believed we had a winning product, yet despite huge efforts couldn't get the main toy distributors to take it on. We had even placed an order for 27,000 copies but we had nowhere to sell it.

Commiserating over a coffee with Whit in a Seattle Starbucks, after failing to get our game placed in the American International Toy Fair, I looked around at the customers in the store and found our answer.

We could bring our games here, to where our customers are, rather than where games are traditionally sold. It was the perfect audience of young, hip professionals. That 'moment' in the coffee shop transformed our destiny.

We persuaded Starbucks to stock the game, the first time they'd sold such an item – and that led to prodigious growth as we approached and sold Cranium to other outlets that had the same types of customer as that coffee shop: Amazon, Barnes and Noble etc.

Later, Whit and I sold our company to Hasbro for $77.5million.

Coffee houses of old have always harboured and celebrated the creative spirit; the writer, the artist, the academic and the activist.

It's the natural place for inspiration and ideas. It was the natural place for us."

Craig Newmark, founder, craigslist and craigconnects

"I got deep into the coffee house thing, getting work done and talking with people."

There are more than 700 local craigslist websites in 70 countries. In the US alone, more than 60 million people use it every month and it receives more than 50 billion page views every month.

"The coffee house trend hit Detroit around 1990 and I embraced it immediately. My head was full of the Beat Generation fantasy, where people got together for serious talk. When I got to San Francisco I got deep into the coffee house thing, getting work done and talking with people.

My first year was in Russian Hill and Royal Ground became my regular place. I made friends I'm still in contact with. Now, I've lived in Cole Valley nearly 20 years, my hangout is a place called Reverie.

The neighborhood is full of tech people, coding away, often going to some lengths to find a signal. To get people to talk with each other, there is no Wi-Fi at Reverie. It's great for people like me.

I really am a nerd with limited social appetite but I do like having people around when I work. The Beat thing lives on, since original coffee houses like Café Trieste survive and I get there sometimes.

Coffee and caffeine is a powerful technology. From 1600s Europe, a network of coffee houses stimulated a lot of emergent behaviour, including the creation and growth of the equities market. They also served as the content distribution network for bloggers like John Locke and Thomas Paine.

That led to the development of representative democracy in the UK and US, and that's my idea of a really big deal."

Michael Acton Smith
creator of Moshi Monsters

"One afternoon in my local Caffè Nero I was doodling monsters. I thought it would be fun to try and bring the little creatures to life."

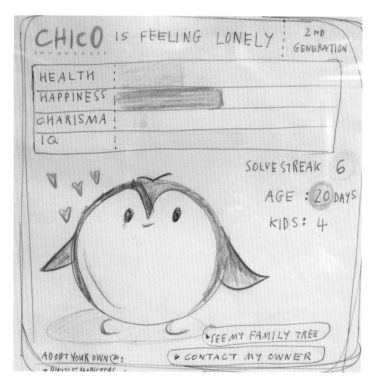

More than 75 million Moshi Monsters have been adopted in over 150 countries worldwide, and over $100 million worth of Moshi Monsters products were sold in 2011. This is that famous first drawing.

"I've always loved working out of coffee shops as it's my perfect environment for getting into a flow state. Most of my breakthrough business ideas have happened in coffee shops with a single macchiato, while scribbling in my sketch book with my Pilot 0.5mm V-ball pen.

One of my biggest ideas came about in the Battersea branch of Caffè Nero on a quiet Sunday afternoon. I'd raised a lot of venture capital for a game I'd developed called Perplex City. Unfortunately the game was too complex and didn't attract a large enough audience.

I still had some of the invested money left so had just enough time to develop a new game before the cash fully ran out. As Perplex City faltered I used to spend increasing amounts of time in the coffee shops of Battersea and Clapham on the weekends, sketching out new ideas for a game.

One afternoon in my local Caffè Nero I was doodling monsters (luckily I had my coloured pencils with me that day) and thought it would be fun to try and bring the little creatures to life. I'd seen the success of Tamagotchi and imagined kids might like to adopt their own monster on the web. That was the kernel of the idea for the game that became Moshi Monsters.

My favourite coffee shop in the world? The armchair by the window on the top floor of the Costa Coffee in Marlow, on the Thames, just outside London."

Jamie Coomarasamy
BBC World Service presenter

"We broadcast the BBC's coverage of Obama's election next to this roaster."

Over 145 million people globally listen to the BBC World Service.

"There are few better locations for a radio broadcast than a café. From Berlin to Beirut, when you're painting an audio portrait, the rattle of cups and the caffeine-fuelled hubbub provide the perfect canvas.

While covering the 2012 US election, I found myself in Wilson's Coffee and Tea in Racine, Wisconsin – a friendly and unpretentious place, where they prepare a palette of artisan coffees on the premises. They are roasted in an impressive contraption, hooked up to a computer that ensures optimal timing and temperatures.

I was marvelling at this machine when my editors called, asking me to present that day's programme from 'the road'. Not long ago, that would have meant setting up a satellite dish outside, but these days a good Wi-Fi connection turns your mobile device into a mobile studio. So, no need to move. The rumble of the roaster would provide the backing track.

As that day's show got underway, a steady trickle of listeners began to arrive, sipping and smiling and keen to chat. They'd tuned in to hear about the world, only to discover it had come to their local coffee shop."

Dennis Crowley
Co-founder and CEO of Foursquare

"In the early days, a handful of coffee shops in the East Village were our offices. They were where Naveen and I decided to start Foursquare and where we built half of the prototype."

More than 30 million people use Foursquare worldwide. There have been more than three billion check-ins, with millions more every day.

1. Cafe OST COFFEE SHOP

441 E 12th St at Ave A, New York, NY

"Naveen and I built half of the original foursquare prototype here (pre-SXSW 2009). This was before I was drinking coffee, so I was downing like 5 hot a day here (someone's gotta pay for that wifi!)"

Dens · August 29, 2011

⬜ Been there   🔖 Save

---

2. Think Coffee COFFEE SHOP

248 Mercer St btwn W 3rd & W 4th St, New York, NY

"Naveen & I built 1/2 of the foursquare prototype here (mostly at the back table near the bathroom). The "mayor" feature in 4SQ came from our buddy Chad making fun of us for camping at that table :)"

Dens · June 13, 2011

⬜ Been there   🔖 Save

---

3. Corner Shop Cafe BREAKFAST SPOT

643 Broadway at Bleecker, New York, NY

"There's been a bunch of diff bars below this cafe. At @lock's bday party in Jan 2009, downstairs is where @Naveen & I decided we should try to replace dodgeball w/ 4SQ & launch it @ SXSW in March."

Dens · August 29, 2011

⬜ Been there   🔖 Save

Tom Watson
British Member of Parliament and Deputy Chair of the Labour Party

How to 'persuade' a UK MP to contribute to your book

 tom_watson @tom_watson   17 hrs
Fake Bishop gatecrashes a pre-conclave meeting of cardinals:
spiegel.de/international/...

 Chris Ward @chrisatcoffice   17 hrs
@tom_watson while you're working away in that coffee shop!
fancy writing those 200 words on how brilliant it is for you!!?

 tom_watson @tom_watson   17 hrs
@chrisatcoffice How do you know I'm in a coffee shop?!
💬 Hide conversation   ↩ Reply

 Chris Ward @chrisatcoffice   16 hrs
@tom_watson the relaxed, creative pose..?! Now, get writing!

 tom_watson @tom_watson   16 hrs
@chrisatcoffice ok, on it.

Tom and I met as we shared something stronger than coffee in Barcelona.
I needed a drink as I had just presented at a conference alongside Julian
Assange of Wikileaks and was still feeling scarily out of my depth!

"I spend a large part of my life in coffee shops. Sometimes I have meetings there. Long-suffering assistants turn up and bring me things. I give them coffee.

Mainly, though, I'm on my own. Or, rather, one of the reasons I'm there is that I'm not on my own. I could sit in an office if I wanted that. I like the gentle buzz, the human traffic, the passionate staff. Because that's something that distinguishes a proper coffee shop: knowledgeable staff who really care. They coax great coffee out of their beloved La Marzocco and Elektra machines with a love and commitment that money can't buy.

My own passion grew out of a paranoia – about being followed during the early days of the phone hacking investigation. Later, it turned out I was indeed put under surveillance by the News of the World's 'Fake Sheikh', Mazher Mahmood. But so randomly was I roaming between coffee shops, while discharging my duties as an advocate, lawmaker and agitator that they never tracked me down. At least I don't think they did.

I spent an entire summer writing in the best independent coffee shop in England – Huddersfield's Coffee Evolution. When their four-cup espresso maker was replaced, I felt like they were burying an old friend.

Fast, free Wi-Fi, good staff, great beans, a comfy armchair and the occasional unobtrusive chat – that's all you need."

Lizzie Bain, co-owner of Ozone Coffee Roasters

"The question I am most asked: what's the Wi-Fi password? Our regulars use us unashamedly as a free office space. We love that – it's how it all began for me. The more iPads, highlighters and textbooks the better. Coffee is the future people!"

"Growing up on the west coast of New Zealand in the '90s, café culture was booming. So it was inevitable that a big chunk of my childhood was spent hanging out in cafés with my sisters doing our homework and supping on our chai lattes. By the time my high school exams came around I was drinking double shot flat whites by the dozen.

On my first night at university in Wellington I took my new room mates to The Lido, the café where my Mum had studied (I'd heard a rumour that Peter Jackson of The Lord Of The Rings fame used to hang out there, so I knew it must be cool enough to take my new friends). It was the start of three years of 'studying' - aka people-watching, daydreaming and drinking coffee. When I wasn't in college I was working as a barista and becoming more obsessed with the coffee industry.

I met James, my English fiancé, when I took a job at the iconic Wellington coffee house, Pravda. This was a business hot house – politicians met for a coffee, Prince William came in for a hot chocolate and hot legal deals were signed.

While I served up coffee, James was busy roasting and training baristas. But London was calling. We wanted to think big and couldn't do it alone. So we called up Craig Macfarlane, owner of Ozone Coffee Roasters in New Zealand and together we hit London.

Three years on, I co-own my own café and coffee roastery in East London."

Ozone is an award-winning company, wholesaling beans in New Zealand. They opened a London roastery and kiwi-style café and supply beans across the UK. It's been named a top 10 place to have brunch in London.

Andrew Brackin, student, hub worker. Founder of Tomorrow's Web meet-ups

"Google has a space called Campus which has a café floor where anyone can work for free. It's great for meetings and getting your head down. Everyone around you is trying to build the next big thing and that's rather inspiring."

"While 16 and studying at sixth form, I created a digital store that had more than 100,000 designer and creative users. I wanted to create a service of value that I could work on for a number of years.

In the Summer of 2012 I finished sixth form and took a chance. I decided to go for it, to try and start a company with nothing.

I couldn't work in an office. They're far too expensive, incredibly uninspiring and there's no social context. No one is working around you. I started working from coffee shops and hybrid co-working spaces to see if this would work for me.

I'm incredibly unproductive at home. Having direct access to great food and drink, good Wi-Fi and seating at Google Campus leads to a productive day for me. I work from Shoreditch, the centre of London's tech scene, because I know that I'll likely bump into someone interesting or make a good contact. This means I can be the most productive but also stay connected and attend events nearby.

After six months, I'm launching the service, have signed on a number of brands and am thinking about the next steps. This is hopefully just the start of another exciting journey."

Mark Dixon, CEO of Regus

"In the future our children will reminisce about daily commuting to the office, in much the same way that we recall life without the mobile."

Regus is the world's largest global provider of flexible workspace, serving more than 800,000 customers every day.

"I was working in a hotel reception in Brussels when I decided to set up Regus. I was frustrated with working out of hotels and they aren't the best place to hold confidential meetings or impress potential customers. I just knew there had to be a better way to work on the road and at home and I didn't think I was the only one. So I found an empty office space in Stephanie Square and within a week I'd leased it.

That was in 1989. Now we provide flexible workspace in over 1500 centres in 100 countries, with Stephanie Square as our number one centre. We have offices, virtual offices, business lounges and more, including in service stations and shops.

Times are changing. Five years ago, 95% of our members worked at a fixed desk Monday to Friday, nine to five. That figure is down to only 20%.

We're no longer tethered to a desk and technology is only going to get better.

Also, more and more business leaders are recognising that flexibility can help work-life balance. They are providing the tools and technology that enable them to measure success from output, not time spent at a desk in an office."

My stories

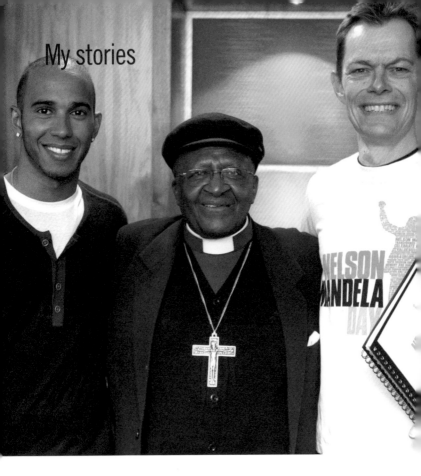

"I ran my website and Mandela Day events from cafés and race day tents as I raced across remote parts of the world."

The Mandela Day Pledge Book launch with my hero, Archbishop Desmond Tutu, Chair of The Elders, and F1 driver Lewis Hamilton, both in London and in the same room at the same time – that was fun making happen!

"After I sold my agencies, I launched a sports website called isporty, with former England football manager Terry Venables. At the same time as I was securing the investment funding and overseeing the small team growing the site, I ran ten marathons and competed in mountain bike races across the Alps, Rockies and South Africa.

This was before the time of a mobile Apple device, so it was a Blackberry that enabled me to operate as if I was back in the office and not, as I actually was, sweating, hurting and lying wiped out in a small tent at the bottom of another mountain pass.

I ran isporty from cafés and the race day tents. I know that it wouldn't have achieved more if I had been sitting in an office twelve hours a day. In fact, taking part in major sports events, while running a website that was trying to engage those very same competitors, meant we probabaly achieved more by being so close to our customers.

The Mandela Day Pledge Book is a campaign we run for the Nelson Mandela Foundation. Again, I was able to appear professional and gain the support of major brands and stars such as David and Victoria Beckham and One Direction as if I was wearing a suit in an office and not skintight Lycra in a tent."

"For the legacy of the South African FIFA World Cup we raised millions of pounds for education by texting a billion people around the world from 80 coffee shops."

Working in a lowly coffee shop doesn't stop you meeting someone in high office! 1 Preparing our presentation in Pacific Coffee, Hong Kong with Mark and Ralph; 2 Johannesburg with President Zuma;
3 A 1GOAL team meeting at the brilliant Café Neo in Cape Town;
4 Johannesburg with U.N Secretary-General Ban Ki-moon.

"The aim of 1GOAL, our legacy campaign for the FIFA 2010 World Cup, was to use the focus on Africa to raise awareness of the need for governments to provide education for all children globally.

An opportunity arose for the global mobile phone industry to support the campaign through their body the GSMA.

Our first aim was to convince their board in Hong Kong, so for a few days we spent endless hours writing and re-writing our presentation in the coffee bars of Kowloon Road. It worked – they came on board and two-thirds of the global mobile phone companies would text their customers with information about 1GOAL and education for all.

That's tens of companies across tens of countries, so off I went to visit them and help coordinate the campaign.

I ended up working away in more than 80 coffee shops from San Francisco to Tokyo and London to Johannesburg. In one very long weekend I worked on the free Wi-Fi in Seoul, Dubai, Tokyo, Cairo, Lagos and Johannesburg. Crazy but worth it.

The mobile phone companies worked their magic and we ended up with a petition of more than 18 million people that was presented by our vice-chairs Queen Rania of Jordan and former UK Prime Minister Gordon Brown at the UN in New York.

The result of the World Cup? Spain won, but also millions more children got to go to school, every single day."

Which hot spot will it be today?

The whole of life in every day

Foxcroft & Ginger. One of my favourite places to work in Soho, London and, coincidentally, directly opposite the office where I ran my last business.

An 'Out of Office' day

Inspiration – and a deadline! – can strike at any time. So there are any number of inspiring hot spots you can check-in at, any time, any day.

There isn't a routine day. This was mine yesterday.

6.40am	– Wake up, look at emails on phone with one eye open
7am	– Catch up on overnight emails in home study
8am	– Breakfast and walk kids to school
9am	– 35-mile cycle training ride
11am	– Stop off at Cinnamon, Windsor, for conference calls
11.30am	– Further 18-mile ride back home
12.30pm	– Change, shower, catch up on calls at home
2pm	– Fernandez & Wells, Soho, lunch and project work
5pm	– Whole Foods, pick up dinner, work at in-store cafe
7pm	– Home, dinner, kids, Brownies, pub
1am	– Procrastinate with the iPad in bed…

The cafe with the best view in London; The Serpentine Bar & Kitchen overlooking the lake in Hyde Park. No Wi-Fi, but serves great beer and welcomes the tourists of the world.

Coffee shops

Cool independent coffee shops, delis and international chains are very positive places. Customers go there to meet friends, to laugh, smile, eat good food, enjoy good conversation and relax.

Does that sound like many offices you've worked in?

With a smartphone, a fresh cappuccino, the 'occasional' muffin, a laptop with Wi-Fi and shared space in that busy coffee shop, you are part of a movement that is changing the face of work forever.

The Government of South Australia using the power of their coffee shops to promote Adelaide to investors and tourists.

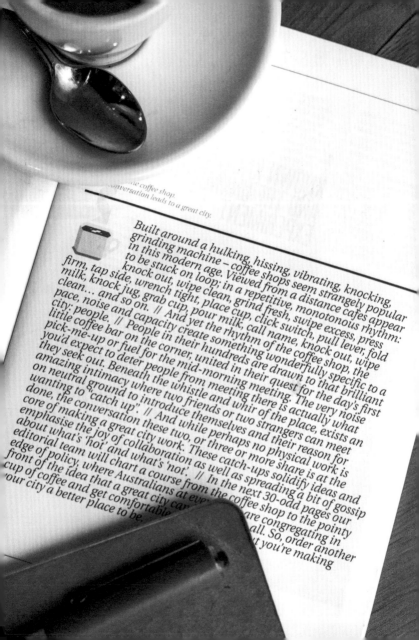

Built around a hulking, hissing, vibrating, knocking, grinding machine – coffee shops seem strangely popular in this modern age. Viewed from a distance cafes appear to be stuck on loop; in a repetitive, monotonous rhythm: knock out, wipe clean, grind fresh, swipe excess, press firm, tap side, wrench tight, place cup, click switch, pull lever, fold milk, knock jug, grab cup, pour milk, call name, knock out, wipe clean… and so on. // And yet the rhythm of the coffee shop, the pace, noise and capacity create something wonderfully specific to a city: people. // People in their hundreds are drawn to that brilliant little coffee bar on the corner, united in their quest for the day's first pick-me-up or fuel for the mid-morning meeting. The very noise you'd expect to deter people from meeting there is actually what they seek out. Beneath the whistle and whir of the place, exists an amazing intimacy where two friends or two strangers can meet on neutral ground to introduce themselves and their reason for wanting to "catch up". // And while perhaps no physical work is done, the conversation these two, or three or more share is at the core of making a great city work. These catch-ups solidify ideas and emphasise the joy of collaboration as well as spreading a bit of gossip about what's 'hot' and what's 'not'. // In the next 30-odd pages our editorial team will chart a course from the coffee shop to the pointy edge of policy, where Australians at ev... are congregating in front of the idea that a great city car... ...all. So, order another cup of coffee and get comfortab... ...t you're making your city a better place to be.

Coffee shops provide everything

Effects of caffeine intake include, increased awareness, shorter, reaction times, & ninja powers

Curators Coffee, Central London.

you could EVER possibly need...

Coffee Tea Room
Cocktail Bar
Food served all day
Free WIFI
Private Rooms
for Parties
Belly Dancer show

Souk Bazaar, Covent Garden, London.

In-house cafés

Many businesses now create their own in-house coffee shops, or even entire campus-like areas.

The leading companies are moving entirely away from structured rows of desks and offices to open-plan studios that resemble playful areas.

This means you can achieve a good halfway house to the complete mobile lifestyle.

You get the buzz of a coffee house but not the chance to work alongside your customers. You do though, get the chance for the random conversations with colleagues that can often result in the solution you are looking for.

> *"Innovation is often the result of random conversations – collisions. We want to accelerate those collisions."*

Tony Hsieh, CEO, Zappos

Google Campus, London.

Hubs and co-working spaces

Hubs are the fastest growing new type of workspace across the globe. Soon we will see one on every high street. They provide co-working spaces with the ambience of a coffee shop and the supporting infrastructure of an office.

They charge per person, per desk, per month. If leaving the office entirely isn't for you straight away or you are starting up and need some infrastructure, then they make the excellent first step.

International digital brands are opening their own hubs as incubators for start-ups, while at the other end of the market, some new coffee shop brands are opening that offer great coffee and full support for 'Out of Office' workers.

The largest office space providers in the world have adapted their whole models to offer flexible solutions, rather than simply traditional office space.

Hub Westminster, Central London. One of 25 hubs on five continents and where some of this book was written.

You

00 /
100% Open Ltd
59Strings
8fold
A+ Architecture
ABC Ltd
Ad IQ
Agency Bell Ltd
Alberto Campo
Alex Watson (R
Andrew Campb
Andrews Outco
Antonio Borges
Aperture & Arc
Apple and Ink L
Armonia UK Tru
Barry's Lounge
Batch 10
BEcause
Bespoke Databa
Beyond Textboo
Big Issue Invest
Big Jon
Blue Dot World
Brand Influence
Brett Scott (The
British Black Bu
Broadmargins L
Cassie Robinson
CE Ventures Inc
Cecilia Wee
Change The Con
Charlie Osmond
Chris Packe
Circle Digital
Cleantech Capita
Clink Wines Ltd
Community Mon
Consortium of B
Covert Promotio
Craftivist Collect
DADAMAC
datascience
David Barrie
David Turner (Sir
Debtxplained
Deci Ltd
Deloitte Social In
Design Council
Design For Social
Dhruv Kumar
Do-Inc
Dr Vladas Lasas L
DragonFruit Ltd
Dromomaniacs
E Garden
Eagle Insight Ltd
Earth Security Ini
eco2
EFFEFF Limited
El Hassan Science
Elaine Callighen
Elio Studio Ltd

Planes, trains and automobiles

Get yourself a good mobile internet deal to use while you travel between hot spots.

On most trains and many planes you will now find Wi-Fi.

It's also about to be made available in the back of every taxi.

Other places I've worked from include:
Hotel receptions
Shisha cafes
McDonald's
Book shops
Gyms

This list will grow and grow as the 'Out of Office' movement grows and businesses compete for your custom.

Rory Sutherland
47 minutes ago via Twitter

My single from Middlesbrough to Whitby is £6.10 for a 90 minute journey. Rather cheap alternative to office space when you think about it.

Rory Sutherland

Wifi on the plane. Will report back when we reach 10000 ft.

Like • Comment • Share • @rorysutherland on Twitter • 2 minutes ago via Twitter

Mike Butcher

Nice to see you! RT @Documentally: Just bumped into @mikebutcher in the airport cafe. That guy will work anywhere.

Like • Comment • Share • @mikebutcher on Twitter • 3 minutes ago via Twitter

Two people at the very top of their professions and generally to be found 'Out of Office'. Rory is Executive Creative Director and Vice-Chairman of OgilvyOne agency, London, and Vice-Chairman of Ogilvy & Mather UK. Mike is the European Editor for TechCrunch, the leading technology website. And if it's good enough for these two, it's good enough for me.

Beds, bathrooms and backrooms

Millions of people work productively from home, using the local coffee shop for their shot of community and inspiration and to escape any feeling of loneliness, or give them a reason to actually get dressed.

Quite often that positive 'flow' moment that gets you working can strike in the middle of the night. You're relaxed, had something to eat (sugar levels are up), watched a bit of TV and suddenly feel inspired and 'ready to go'. But it's pitch black – and unless you live in our ever-growing number of 24-hour cities, you will be working from home.

So stock up with an AeroPress – the best home coffee maker – and some fresh beans and enjoy the productive midnight hours. You should try and get up a bit later the following morning though, and not feel guilty about doing so.

> *"To judge by the ideas generated there, many beds have a better right to be called offices than offices."*

Alain de Botton

> *"21% of the British population admit to checking their emails while on the toilet"*

YouGov survey

Alain de Botton is the brilliant philosopher. Daily, he tweets simple lifechanging thoughts relevant to our everyday life. He has also written the ultimate book on this subject, The Pleasures and Sorrows of Work.

"Having lunch together is so much more important to creating something than a business meeting."

Jack Dorsey, founder, Twitter and Square

The pastries at Fernandez & Wells, Somerset House, London are, as they say, to die for.

Science may never come with a better communication system than the

Written large on the wall at The Royal Institution of Great Britain

up

office

cation

coffee

break Earl Wilson

The medicinal benefits of caffeine

The great Flat Cap Coffee in the City of London, appealing to the aspirations of the pin striped city workers.

are numerous

Curators Coffee, using genuine statistics to compete with their near neighbours Flat Cap!

The very best inspiration...

For warmth. The best hot chocolate (with white rum!) at the Wi-Fi cafe in Chamonix.

For higher intervention! In the garden at Buckingham Palace. Coffee not great but nice gaff.

The perfect coffee. 'The God Shot'. Found only once, in Berlin.

From history, Groppi's in the backstreets of Cairo.

...I've found around the world

For rewarding hard work. The shack at the top of Sa Calobra bike ride in Majorca.

For on-the-go. The best can of coffee. The Boss – straight out of a Tokyo vending machine.

For a change. 'Potato Latte' in Seoul. It wasn't great.

For the perfect sugar & alcohol kick: Chocolate & Guinness cake, around London.

The best infographic that represents how smart workers act.

The WorkSn
CODE OF

OI!

1 Don't yell into your headset like you're at a construction site

∞

4 No making Skype calls without a headset

5 If you see someone in greater need, give up or share your table

So, you're a laptop-toting, cappuccino-sipping, free-range mobile worker. We know it can be rewarding, but Lordy it can also be a trial!

That's why WorkSnug, Plantronics and Nokia have crowd-sourced a 'Code of Conduct' for mobile workers – a guide on how best to behave when working in coffee shops.

Each rule in the code has been submitted and voted for by the WorkSnug community.

×1

8 If there are two power sockets available, only use one of them!

WorkSnug connects mobile workers to the nearest & best places to work www.worksnug.com.

Follow us on Twitter @WorkSnug. Download our free mobile app: www.worksnug.com/apps.

Thanks t
coffee-sip
contribu

Coffee Shop ONDUCT

WorkSnug plantronics. NOKIA

3 Don't talk or text whilst being served. It's rude!

RUDE!

No nursing a single cup of coffee for hours whilst hogging the best sofa

@
TWITTER
FACEBOOK

7 Be polite to the staff

THANKS!

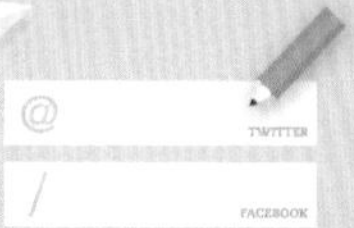

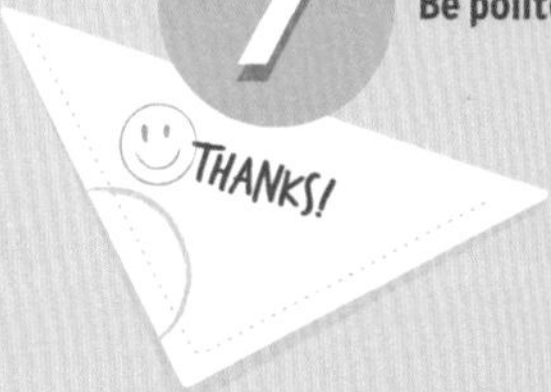

6 Help promote the coffee shop you're working in – tweet, like or check-in.

9 Remember, you're sharing the space with other people – this is not your personal space!

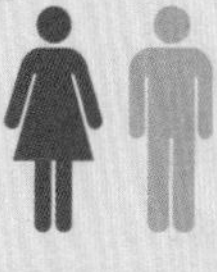

10 No hogging the bandwidth!

fi-hoppin',
e workers who
ode.

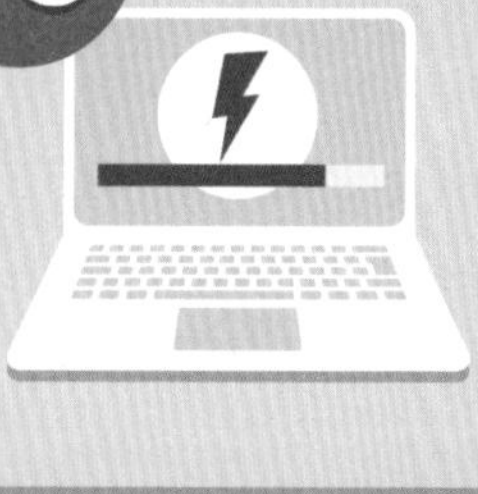

N°. OF VOTES

6044

MAP OF VOTES

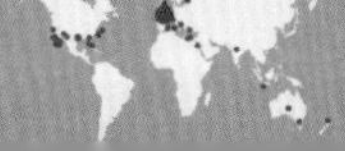

FLAT CAP COFFEE

The Powers of a man's mind are directly proportioned to the quantity of coffee he drinks.

Sir James Mackintosh

the borough barista

"chocolate, men,
coffee — some
things are better
rich"

PENNY U

Everything you need to know
For the price of a cup of coffee

The term 'Penny University' originates from 18th Century cafés in London.

For one penny, you could enter a café and get free coffee, the newspapers and the latest gossip from runners, who were like reporters, going round cafés making announcements.

These cafés were also where you could find people from all levels of society, which was rare in a world where class was still so important. Anyone who had a penny could enter. University students often spent more time in cafés than at school.

With the wide range of conversations, from political to intellectual, students came out of the cafés feeling more intelligent or knowledgeable than if they'd gone to school.

You could acquire an education for the price of a cup of coffee.

The same holds true today.

The Penny University Prospectus

"The illiterate of the 21st century will not be those who cannot read and write, but those who cannot learn, unlearn and relearn."

Alvin Toffler

The real teachers for us coffee-drinking, Penny University 'students', are the new cutting-edge authors who lead the way in future thinking. They guide us away from the rat race mentality of the 20th century and show us the new lifestyle that's possible in a digital world.

Their teachings about how to live an 'Out of Office' life, where you can achieve both a successful career and a life lived to the full, will eventually make up the textbooks of tomorrow.

I left school with one qualification. Everything I learnt of value came from my parents, working as a shop assistant and reading these Penny University books.

Welcome to Penny University: school of life.

If you need to come up with a great idea, never, ever, hold a brainstorm

genius, but Cain points ou Apple would never have ex without the solitary work Steve Wozniak, the engine who created the personal con puter that inspired Jobs to found the company.

In his memoir, Wozniak wrote: "Most inventors and engineers I've met are like me ... they live in their heads. They're almost like artists. In fact, the very best of them are artists. And artists work best alone."

Before he started Apple, Wozniak designed calculators at Hewlett-Packard. Every day at 10am and 2pm a trolley laden with doughnuts and

Steve Wozniak is the co-founder of Apple. This is my favourite quote in the whole book because it's 100% true of so many people I know.

Have the best ideas in a coffee shop

A coffee shop is one of the very best places to come up with new ideas.

In 1965, James Webb Young identified a five-part process that leads to the eureka moment. The key part is having the time and space, mixed with external inspiration, in order to let a new idea solidify in your mind. An office, study or studio cannot provide this – a coffee shop can.

A Technique for Producing Ideas
by James Webb Young. Professionals from poets and painters to scientists and engineers have used the techniques in this book to generate exciting ideas at any time, on any subject.

Work when you feel like it…

When you are working well, feeling vibrant, having good ideas, producing a great piece of work without interruptions and getting things done fast and effectively, you are 'in the flow'.

"People who are in 'flow' achieve a state of consciousness that is in harmony with their surroundings and feelings. They do not make distinctions between work and play. They create an inner state of being that brings them peace and fulfilment. They are focused, what they do is meaningful and has purpose, they are absorbed in their activities and they have a sense of connection to their inner self and also with others. Some people experience it for minutes, some for hours, some for days on end…"

How often do you feel that good in an office?

How often do you feel that good 'Out of Office'?

Flow
by Mihaly Csikszentmihalyi. Read the latest edition of this excellent book to discover how you can control flow and not just leave it to chance.

...but stop working as soon as you don't feel like it

Be prepared to work odd hours. Enlightening thoughts and the feeling of flow can be like a dream. It appears and disappears, sometimes without warning, so you must be ready to seize the moment, whether that's at 7.30am on a Monday morning or 9pm on a Sunday evening.

Work opening hours, not office hours.

People working while in a state of flow are able to achieve their work in around half the time it would take them in a normal office state.

The big trick, though, is to stop working as soon as you realise you are not in the flow anymore and go and do something completely different – and fun!

You are are not being productive anymore but you're not tied to the desk. You don't have to send more emails, or look at more pictures of cats.

You are in control and can go and do whatever you like.

Enjoy it and don't feel guilty. The feeling of flow will be back shortly.

Only do what you do best

Anyone can get what they want, from anywhere in the world, in a few moments. The only factors influencing if they get it from you or one of your competitors are whether you are cheapest or the best.

I know which I prefer to compete on.

But to be the best, you don't have time to work on anything other than that. You may already know what it is you are prepared to spend 10,000 hours on becoming the best at and if you want to really enjoy life, make it something you love doing. You can create a value from it that you can sell to other people; teaching, consulting, competing, writing or selling it.

Working in a coffee shop you are out of sight, avoiding all the interruptions that stop you becoming the best at what you do: time-draining meetings, random requests and the dreaded cc of your name on emails.

Outliers
Malcolm Gladwell on how and why people spend 10,000 hours on becoming the best.

What Would Google Do?
Jeff Jarvis highlights the unique opportunities that arise if you concentrate on being the best at one thing.

Keep flexible

You really cannot plan or predict genuine, huge success. If we could, then we would all be successful. Marketing campaigns are carefully planned but only about one in ten, at best, achieve what they set out to.

The opportunity to achieve success mostly comes from somewhere unpredictable. To seize it, you need to be flexible enough to react quickly.

That happened with both the Friends Reunited website and Red Nose Day. Both suddenly leapt forward in popularity due to us being able to respond to a piece of media coverage that focused on an area we hadn't predicted.

Big opportunities come with the demand for an immediate response! They blow away your carefully structured plans but if you don't respond instantly they disappear as quickly as they arrive.

Being 'Out of Office' gives you the advantage over big businesses and agencies who miss these opportunities because they can't react quickly enough.

The Lean Startup
Eric's Reis's book explains how to make better, faster decisions and waste less time and money.

Share

Halve your problems AND double your chance of success!

Ownership is going the same way as the office – it's not required and the status is fast disappearing. Ownership causes problems; costs spiral up, while value spirals down.

You share your social life, now share everything else.

Share the things you've bought.
The average lawn mower is used 4 hours a year, power drill for only 20 minutes in its entire lifespan and the average car is unused for 22 hours a day. Share.

Share ideas.
Share your new ideas to see if people are interested and towards building an improved version. It's way cheaper than building and paying for a whole prototype.

Share everything you do online.
If you create or build anything for the web do it only if both you and your customers will share it.

Share a coffee and your gear in a coffee shop.
You never know where a conversation or favour will lead.

What's Mine Is Yours
Rachel Botsman and Roo Rogers
have written the bible for the sharing economy.

Find most answers right in front of your eyes...

Too many people are distracted from seeing and enjoying the world right in front of their eyes by deadlines and demands. They think that finding the answers are harder than they actually are, that they need to look further afield to find a solution. Not true!

When you were a child you had a sense of wonder about the world right in front of you. Many people lose that but you need to retain or regain it if you don't want to miss the big opportunities that are right in front of your eyes, every single day.

> *"Life is what happens to you while you're busy making other plans."*

John Lennon

Life is what goes on 'Out of Office', while you are busy in the office.

I found the answer to reuniting with my wife...

Helen and I were splitting up, so looking for a job certainly wasn't at the front of my mind when I was reading the morning paper. For me, though, reading a newspaper means being open to everything in it because you never know what will inspire you, even in the job ads when I'm not looking for a job!

That day, I saw an advert for Creative Communications Director at Comic Relief, one of the UK's best-loved charities. I applied, and while being interviewed by its founder, writer and film director Richard Curtis, I discovered that we shared many beliefs in 'Out of Office' working. Enough I think, to help me get the job.

My mood changed considerably for the better. My wife was impressed by my renewed enthusiasm and it played its part in reuniting us.

...and the answer to reuniting millions of people

While running my marketing agency I read a small article about a great start-up website called Friends Reunited. I thought it was a great idea, and while reading a review of a TV programme I hadn't seen, I came up with the idea of how to make it successful.

The reviewer criticised the show for featuring some street-savvy, suited entrepreneurs who were planning to spend millions from selling their website before they had even launched it.

That sparked the idea of marketing Friends Reunited as if it was purely an 'Out of Office' business, run by a couple from home, without an office or a suit in sight. I couldn't see the public wanting to pay those suited dudes £5 to join a website, but they would trust and identify with Steve and Julie.

It worked a storm, as 12 million people in the UK joined up.

The postman beat a daily path to the Pankhursts' front door with bags of membership cheques, and TV crews to the back door to interview Julie for the cosy, home-run business story.

Think bigger than you are now
Think in millions

This approach was confirmed to me over a coffee in New York with author and TED speaker Simon Sinek. We had only been introduced because, in the words of our mutual acquaintance, "Chris thinks like you – in millions."

We agreed that most people only think about how they are going to achieve their next sale. But you can leave your competitors behind by simply thinking bigger than them. There's a lot less competition for a million sales.

It takes as much work to sell ten products to a small customer as it does to sell a hundred to a larger one. So try selling a million to an even bigger one.

Whole sectors are changing overnight, to the extent that a market leader can become out of date almost instantly. And because of their office tanker full of infrastructure, will find it harder than you to sail into the gap that the developing market has opened up.

You can take them on head to head from home, a hub or the coffee shop. You can think the same as them but you can act ten times faster.

Live life in beta

Being a perfectionist is a creative person's worst nightmare.

Luckily, both Facebook and Google have taught us that to be successful, not everything needs to be perfect.

In fact to succeed you need to share your ideas before they are fully formed so that everyone can become an involved part of the process towards creating an improved version of your idea.

They even created a term for releasing imperfect ideas – beta – so that we perfectionists could launch something against our own better judgments!

This is the beta version of this book.

Espresso Saves lives

Kaffeine in central London, winner of multiple awards, including best independent coffee shop in Europe. Also serves life-saving espresso.

Do good

We are at a defining moment where, through social media, everyone can be judged by their customers and the verdict instantly shared. If you are doing something great, everyone can know about it instantly. It will result in your customers spending more with you and your team staying with you longer.

The opposite is also true of course!

The most successful leaders in the future will be those who are the most socially responsible.

Do something you, your team and your customers love and are proud of.

Screw Business As Usual
It is time to turn capitalism upside down. Richard Branson shows how we can bring more meaning to our lives and help change the world at the same time.

Learn the new three Rs

Be Real in everything you do.

There are so many social media channels where people will share their opinion of you. If you are not authentic, people will soon tell each other, very publicly, which will generally end with you in a worse place. Be honest.

Be Relevant in everything you say.

Queen Rania of Jordan, our 1GOAL campaign Co-Chair, tweeted this for the campaign. Twice as many people retweeted the top fact, which is relevant to everybody's daily life, than the bottom one.

1GOAL @join1goal   10 hrs
Queen Rania: Need $11bn to get every child in developing world into primary school, same amount US spends on pets in 3 months

1GOAL @join1goal   10 hrs
Queen Rania: If you educate a child he/she is 50% less likely to get HIV/AIDS. http://bit.ly/3uQDV2 (via @ClintonTweet) join1goal.

Do it - Right now.

Realtime is the new primetime.

Office workers traditionally talk about what was on primetime TV around the office water cooler but Twitter and Facebook are the new global water coolers. It's where the latest conversations are taking place and where people need to be talking about you.

Trending stories have hundreds of thousands of newly-tweeted conversations every single minute. Take advantage of the fact that this is the new primetime: it's free and it's where people will hear the stories about you.

Be real and relevant and do it right now.

> *"To me Twitter is like working in an office with thousands of funny/clever people who only speak when they have something useful or funny or interesting to say."*

Graham Linehan, writer of Father Ted and The IT Crowd.

Penny University life lessons
How to live life to the full

Believe in yourself

With my one qualification I left school to work as a shop assistant in a chemist store. I went from that to eventually selling the two businesses I founded and helping raise good money for great causes. If I didn't believe in myself I would still be that shop assistant.

I've bought a copy of this inspirational book for everyone who has worked for me. Paul Arden is a creative genius.

It's Not How Good You Are, It's How Good You Want to Be by Paul Arden. This is the handbook of how to succeed in the world, a pocket bible to help make the unthinkable and the impossible, possible.

Count success by your happiness not by money

Like many people I was brought up to believe that my life's work, success and happiness would be measured by the amount of money I earned.

I put off happiness and ruined relationships chasing this lie. It took me until I was about 40 to realise I was chasing the wrong goal.

Measure your success by how happy you are, through treasured memories and friends, not through what you think will be treasured possessions.

Happier: Can You Learn To Be Happy?
This book outlines one of Harvard University's most popular and life-changing courses. Tal Ben-Shahar's insightful and inspiring lecture that money is for measuring the success of businesses not people.

Live the life you want today, not tomorrow

Don't wait until retirement to start spending more time with friends and family – do it now, every day.

People in remission from cancer very often say they now realise what's important and go on to spend every day living life to the full. The first thing they seem to realise is that more money is not important and to attend less meetings!

When I sold my companies I was earning a lot of money. I could have walked into a prime job elsewhere but I didn't. I went out and bought a lot of Lycra and spent the next five years marathon running, bike racing and doing homework with my kids! In a way those years cost me millions but I wouldn't change them for the world.

Working 'Out of Office' saves you hours. Use them to live the life you want.

The 4-Hour Workweek
Tim Ferriss's book shares the secrets of the people who have abandoned the "deferred-life plan" and mastered a new way of living.

Do things, don't buy things

Our motivation to work is often simply so that we can afford to buy more branded stuff with our salary. Stuff that is produced to make us believe it will fill an empty feeling deep inside us. To make us feel cooler, faster or more attractive.

If you read these Penny University books you will find that hole will never be filled by buying stuff, so if money is your motivation, you do not need to be tied to a desk when you could be living the life you want now.

With our four kids, we spend more on eating out than on buying things. They don't totally appreciate that yet but going to their favourite family restaurant or my favourite coffee shop means we end each week happily playing with each other, rather than them playing with more digital 'stuff'.

Like many people living an 'Out of Office' lifestyle, it's more important to me how I spend my time than how I spend my money.

Matthew 6.19, The Bible
I am agnostic but I find this verse surprisingly relevant to today. "Don't store up treasures here on earth, where moths eat them and rust destroys them, and where thieves break in and steal. Store your treasures in heaven [I take that as being memories in your head], where moths and rust cannot destroy, and thieves do not break in and steal. Wherever your treasure is, there the desires of your heart will also be".

Never sacrifice friends and family to chase success

I was born in a time when fathers were not tactile with their children. It resulted in me spending 40 years trying to prove to my father I was good enough for him to love me, by being an obnoxious 24/7 desk-bound entrepreneur. I put off friendships in pursuit of the recognition I had craved from my father.

I was wasting my time.

This book explains why that was the case. It shows that due to the adverse effects of a modern childhood, many children do not naturally receive the unconditional love in the first months of their life that they need to grow up with enough self-confidence.

They then waste years chasing the empty feeling it leaves by buying into alcohol, drugs, branded goods, religion... or being an entrepreneur.

My father always loved me, but like many others of the time, he just didn't show it so well.

The Continuum Concept
by Jean Liedloff. This book changed my life. If you can't ever stop working, read this. You'll see how you could be needlessly sacrificing everything else just to prove yourself.

SMART NETWORK.

APP DEVELOPER.

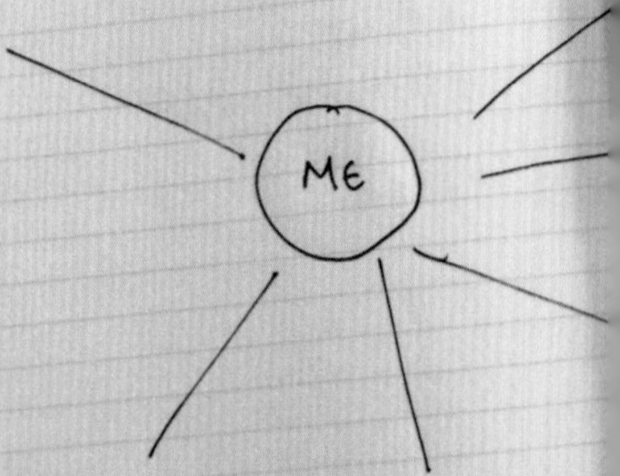

WHITE LABEL CREATOR

COLLABORATORS

ME

THE BRAINS.

MONEYPENNY

THE DOUBLE SHOT

Don't buy infrastructure
Build a network

An office-only based organisation is inflexible, burdened with infrastructure, expensive, in short-term contact with its customers but holding long-term contracts with employees.

An 'Out of Office' network is totally mobile, economical and app-based. It has short-term contracts with highly skilled collaborators and long-term contact with its customers.

If you are doing what you do best, then your network should consist of people who are each doing the same – the one job you need them to do, brilliantly.

Who is playing each role in your network?

Twitter does only what it does best
Its network does the rest

Twitter started as a simple texting service. Many of the popular features that actually turned it into the pulse of the planet, such as retweeting and hashtags, were instigated by its users. It has been estimated that a hundred times as many people contributed to the site than actually worked for the business, none of whom needed a salary or desk.

"*Twitter has remained shockingly simple. We have been at this long enough to realise that simplicity is core to the philosophy.*"

Biz Stone, co-founder of Twitter

"*By encouraging users to experiment with the service and build around it, Twitter cultivated an engaged and loyal user base. Letting developers create a presence on the web that was many times larger than twitter.com was extremely smart.*"

Loic Le Meur, founder of Le Web

1. The white label creator

They have already built what you need so use theirs.

A white label is a product or service produced by another company that you can brand to make it appear as your own.

Don't ever build any digitial functionality when you can happily utilise white label versions to do the job for you, for free.

If you can't find something you need, then that's what you should build as your next business idea!

2. The app developer

In their apps, developers provide all the tools you need to communicate with both your network and customers.

'Out of Office' workers are better equipped than office ones, as Google and Apple lead the way in producing more hardware and software for laptop users than desktop workers.

> *"When you're a digital native, it seems natural to work over IM and email."*

Pete Cashmore
Founder, CEO mashable.com

From founding mashable.com, the social media news website, in his Scottish bedroom in 2005, until 2010, Pete Cashmore didn't meet any of the people that worked for him.

It seems to have worked. Mashable.com now has around 50million page views every month and is one of the most popular websites in the world.

3. The collaborators

You could build your entire success on working with three types
of collaborators. You need to provide them with a platform
where they can show off their own work and feel that they are
adding value.

Citizens
Treat them as an active part of your work, not simply as a
passive potential customer. Their contribution is free. Where
can they add it?

> *"The overlooked lesson of Barack Obama's
> campaign is that it treated voters as citizens with
> active roles in a democratic society, rather than
> passive consumers swayed by party marketing."*

The Guardian

Crowd-sourced volunteers
They will help you if they get something back in return; a leg-
up in their career or recognition.

Contributors
To make a difference, you want the real specialists in your area
to contribute to your work. If you provide a credible platform
they will use it to show off to their fellow experts.

4. The smart geek

Behind every great smart worker is an even smarter brain.

The mindset of many 'Out of Office' workers is often more creative than analytical. But to achieve success, you need every single aspect to be perfect – every 'i' dotted, every 't' crossed.

Find someone you know who is trustworthy and loyal, who can turn everything you do into gold. Someone who is geeky about the finer details and could well still enjoy working in a quiet office.

5. Moneypenny

Often the most enthusiastic member of your network. The person who happily does all the tasks that no one else has time for. They are the glue that holds the network together and are the motor that keeps it moving forward every day.

6. The double shot

The person who can open the doors to the inner circle.

You're an expert but get someone on board who knows ten times more about your sector than you. They can guide you in what to do and get you heard by the influential inner circle that runs it.

It could be a public relations specialist, journalist or an industry figure who becomes your chair or spokesperson. Their involvement will mean the most important people will take you seriously, so it is worth giving them a small stake in your idea.

I've previously secured the expertise of some of the very best people in their respective fields: Stewart Till CBE (Chairman of the British Film Council), Terry Venables (ex-England football manager) and Mike Lee OBE (Director of comms for the London 2012 Olympic bid). I also worked with Richard Curtis CBE (writer and director) at Comic Relief and Queen Rania of Jordan on 1GOAL.

They all opened doors at the highest level, made things happen and enabled our team to walk through and execute the projects.

Queen Rania of Jordan, Co-Chair of our FIFA World Cup 2010, 1GOAL campaign and a leading advocate of education for all.

8 Be the best team player
Ten tips for maintaining great working relationships

Number ten is go for something stronger than a coffee.

Five tips for maximum productivity

Thankfully, this is not about leaning over shoulders while people work! Working with a team from 'Out of Office' is different to running a company.

The main thing is your team need to believe in you and why you are all doing what you are doing.

1. Phone, don't email
    Working remotely you are out of sight. It means your personality won't be seen or heard. If you don't manage it well you could become just another name at the end of another email. You need to ring fellow workers and let them hear you talk, laugh and explain your crazy requests.

2. Take their phone calls
    We all know how easy it is not to take a phone call. A quick glance at the screen and a press of the mute button and it's gone. But don't do that with your team. Your relationships with them will only grow ever more distant every time you do.

3. Get together
    You need to meet regularly with each person. Again, you need to show, like them, you are a full participating member of the team and taking everything everyone says on board.

4. Turn up first

   Many 'Out of Office' workers seem to be by nature late for meetings (I am!). Don't be. We work best with an adrenaline rush and leaving late to get to a meeting means we can feel that rush every day while we chase across town. Do everything against your nature though, for the sake of your relationships and be on time for meetings. Even make it your business to be the first there every week, that will surprise a few people and might be your biggest achievement of the day.

5. Don't email them when they're asleep

   It might impress the boss but it doesn't impress co-workers. They like, just as much as you do, to begin each day with a bit of a plan of what they are going to achieve, not start it with 20 emails from you sent randomly between 11pm last night and 9am this morning.

   Collate your thoughts into one long email during those night-time hours, check it is all still relevant in the morning and send it after 9am. They'll show their appreciation by being fully behind you in the many hours you're not there!

   Anything you want to mail colleagues, always consider ringing them about first though.

Three tips to achieve success

Your team will score one goal after another for you. If you show them where it is.

If you want someone in your network to achieve their best work then you need to provide them with three things.

1. A single goal you believe they can achieve.

2. A reasonable timeframe in which to achieve it, much shorter than you would give them in the office, when they would be distracted and pulled into wider team activity and brainstorms.

3. A promise that you will get back to them quickly with your feedback. As well as helping them, it also provides you with a measure as to whether they are succeeding or not.

Two times to work together

1. The critical moment.

   This is often at the release of your product or the culmination of a campaign, when success is dependent on a short burst of high intensity team work when all interaction and decisions need urgent attention.

   You'll know when it is that time because when you are together you will sound like a café: loud, vibrant, busy and positive. You could use a co-working hub for this period and use the coffee shop for a double shot of inspiration.

2. For a drink, so relationships stay strong.

9 Create the best ideas
With the help of everyone around you

"I know how to sell to your customers, all day, every day."
The Barista

My one qualification wasn't enough to even know about university, let alone go to one. But while doing my first job as a sales assistant, I learned more about what has enabled me to be successful than through any schooling. I learned how to sell to people, face to face.

Baristas do that day in, day out, and it is the one skill you are going to need if you are going to be successful.

"They achieve it without pressurising customers. They explain the benefits of everything and convince them to buy. They know how to negotiate, to deal with the procrastinating customer, to maintain confidence and self-esteem in the face of rudeness, to communicate effectively with a wide range of people and to build long-term relationships. They don't have a huge ego or a huge personality."

When they believe their product is the best, they don't even need to sell. They just communicate.

Go on, ask if they will let you help out behind the counter and gain first hand experience. Failing that, watch closely as they sell, day in, day out, to the same people you want to sell to.

My favourite barista is Chris at Artisan in West London who powers me up each day with an excellent espresso.

"We'll tell you what stops us hearing about most new ideas"
The adults

If it's not important to their lives, people only half listen.

They scan the news and often only understand part of a story but it's enough for them to use for a brief gossip. Then they get down to discussing the important things: their own lives, not your new idea.

They often get the facts of a story scarily wrong. The UK Government actually responded to this problem by issuing the same news up to five times to ensure it did get heard.

Sitting next to people in a coffee shop, you literally see first hand what current issues are preventing them from listening and how wrong their understanding of national issues can be.

To get them talking about your idea, make sure it's relevant to their lives and solves a problem for them. Make it simple so they can easily explain it to their friends. Because if you are going to succeed that's exactly what you need them to do.

"We've found people will give us 30 to 60 seconds to connect with the things they need and love."

Steve Yankovich,
VP, eBay Mobile

"We're dictating the future, whether you like it or not!"
Their kids

Don't ignore those kids shouting loudly about the new game they're playing on their mum's phone. Listen to them because they're not reading about the future, they're dictating it. Many of them will go on to actually code it!

You can probably remember how different the world was until the digital revolution and how fast things are now changing but they don't.

They are digital natives, whose starting point in life is getting everything they want, on demand and free: their favourite music, TV programmes, games, as well as unrestricted access to their friends.

If you want real success you need to secure the expertise of someone dictating the future. Well, they are already here in the coffee shop and providing it to listeners, for free!

Will those kids want your product now, later or never? Will it be superseded? How are they playing and communicating differently to you? What opportunities does that open up?

How they communicate is the future of your business.

"Dad, you had a computer before the internet. What on earth for?"

> *"The 24 year old coming out of Stanford will have a view of technology that the 29 year old, who was 24 just five years ago, would never think of. We love that."*

Marc Andreessen.
Board director of Facebook and eBay among many others achievements

> *"Short-form content to me is long-form to another audience."*

Robert Kyncl, VP and Head of Content, YouTube

"Contribute to the book I'm writing and it will help us both succeed."
The writer

The writer in the corner of your best coffee shop, closest to the coolest companies and magazines you want to be in, is likely to be writing for a newspaper or blogging (and hoping it leads to a book!) about the future trends that will impact you.

They are there for the same reason as you, to be inspired by the relevant people around them.

These are the new lecturers of Penny University, imparting the very latest knowledge and wisdom to all those apprentices keen to learn. Just, they're doing it from a blog rather than a lectern.

Your ideas, combined with their knowledge, could give you all the advantage you need to succeed.

Don't underestimate how important what you think could be to them. So share your thoughts with their blog, so there is still time for you to appear in the book! It could be the best move you make.

"I'll tell you what people are talking about around the world, for free."

The journalists

To stay on top of every opportunity, you need to know what people are talking about over the coffee tables around the world, not just in your own area. You could hear about the latest trends, gossip or cultures in another country or sector that would be unique if you adapt to your own idea.

You won't find what you really need in the paid-for broadsheets and tabloids, though. What you want is covered much better in the free newspapers and supplements that concentrate on the zeitgeist and entertainment talking points rather than the news.

In the morning on your way around town, stop off and throw a free newspaper in your bag. Flick through it later while enjoying your first caffeine hit.

You hear within hours what people are talking about in coffee shops anywhere in the world. So many of my ideas have come through hearing about something in another sector, even another country and adapting it for my own.

"We'll share all our knowledge and experience with you."

The other customers with laptops

Go hang out in the coffee shops where the bosses, execs and bloggers you want to reach have escaped their offices to share coffee, plans and PowerPoints with each other.

This is where you can immerse yourself in the culture of your sector. You can pick up relevant leaflets, start to meet fellow 'Out of Office' workers in the same field, get introduced to important people, get invited to events, get asked to play a role or even get your big break.

Tearing something out to read later? Think twice

Do you tear cuttings out and actually rarely bother to read them later anyway? That's because you've already seen the valuable bits; the context in which you've seen the news, rather than the news itself.

Who wrote it? In which paper? Tabloid, right wing, left wing, broadsheet? What section is it in; news, gossip or business? Is there a photo? Is it full page, colour, and of whom? The opening paragraph or two outline the critical facts and its position on the page shows how important it is.

That all actually only takes a moment to take in and adds up to the answer as to whether the information is valuable to you or not.

Mark Zuckerberg identified that it is who you receive news from, rather than the news itself, that is important and made it the whole premise behind the creation and success of Facebook.

Having a cool magazine nearby is great for an inspiring flick through between bouts of working flow.

Make sure you mix with positive thinkers

Should I kill myself, or have a cup of coffee?

— Albert Camus

Enjoy each day and don't rush. You're no longer in a rat race

It is much easier to be successful if you have a unique idea that is relevant to what everyone is already talking about in every coffee shop.

Therefore it is better to take the time to create a unique idea than spend that same period working on one that has to compete on being the best or cheapest.

I launched an agency marketing to students because we read reports that the Government was aiming for a tenfold increase in the number of young people going to university within eight years. For that time we surfed the crest of the wave as the market grew and everyone from Radiohead to Red Bull wanted us to help them reach the newly important student market.

My business partner jumped off that wave and started surfing a bigger one. He came to our wedding in 1994 and said he was going to start an internet agency. I asked what the internet was exactly, sounded like CB radio to me! But guess which of us has had more business success now?

Remember, though, the best idea is probably right in front of your eyes, in the everyday lives of coffee shop customers. Keep your mind open to all the inspiration and opportunities.

(10) Maximise sales
By helping everyone around you

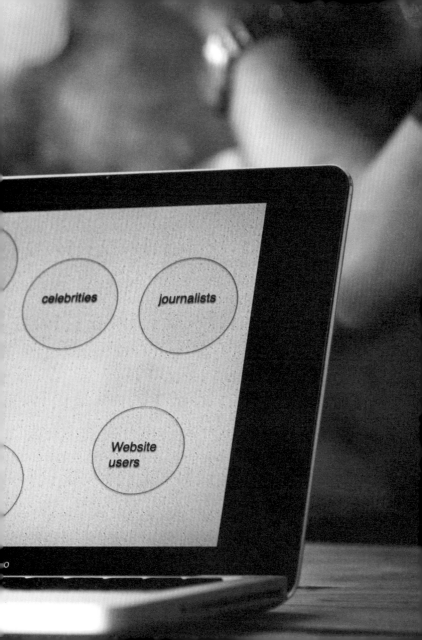

Find your customers in every coffee shop

If you put everything you learn from Penny University into creating your idea, you will end up with a great product and with a market of people who want it because you've lived and learned daily from the very people you want to buy it.

You should be in a position where selling your idea is like selling shoes. Size nine feet? You need size nine shoes. A perfect fit.

But how do you get from the first customer to the millionth?

You need people to talk about it to their friends, to create word of mouth around the coffee tables throughout the country, as successful people have been doing for hundreds of years.

Some people have more friends than others. They are the ones that can spread your message the fastest to their 'friends' in every coffee shop.

To get that to happen you need to help them.

The results of being loyal to perhaps one too many coffee shops.

Help the cool dudes
be followed

Opinion formers are those cool people who want to be the first to tell others about anything new or innovative. Many of them are like us, working next to us, on laptops in coffee shops. Many people think they are so cool that they are the hardest people to engage, that they are too independently minded.

They are actually the easiest people to get talking about your new idea.

Their followers look to them to provide the very latest cutting edge news that they can then impress their own friends with. So they are constantly on the lookout for things that will help them gain their greatest achievement, to 'trend'.

Help solve this problem for them by using the latest innovative technology, either in your idea itself or in the way you communicate it.

Many authors are now discovered online by hard-to-impress publishing houses or agents. Success using innovative blogging platforms is helping pique their interest.

The publicity for this new book contained a good review from chat show host Jonathan Ross, not from TV or radio but from his Twitter account.

Help the laptop users find you

As we know, the public won't go out of their way to find out about you. You have got to become part of their daily lives or you will be completely invisible to them.

Online, you need to provide what you want your audience to see on the websites they are already on. Don't just try and get them to come to your site because they won't.

It's better that they see just one relevant call to action than try and get them to view everything you've got.

With Red Nose Day, we found that not many people clicked through from the BBC's website to our own charity site. So we created widgets that appeared on the BBC site, providing just the critical calls to action that we really wanted them to respond to.

Again, it's a by-product of 'Out of Office' working that you can find out what websites you should be on as you can see first hand what your customers are interested in today, and that won't necessarily be the same as yesterday or tomorrow.

Help the mobile users
Give them something good to share, once a day, every day

With hundreds of friends and followers online, social media junkies haven't got much spare headspace with which to notice you. Information is rushing past them 24/7.

If you can engage them, initially it will be by them rubbernecking you (as when car drivers slow down briefly to look at a car crash and then pass, speed back up and put it behind them). So you've got to keep creating something that stops them in their tracks, every single day of your campaign, to eventually generate an unstoppable momentum.

The green revolutionaries in Iran created a huge global swirl of support with citizens and media but then it all suddenly stopped. Why? Michael Jackson died and the news agenda moved on and didn't return. It hardly ever does.

Don't start too early but once you go – go! Start with a bang and build the momentum every single day with brilliant, short shareable stories. It means no more time for reflection and relaxing, it's go, go, go. Once you have a momentum going you can't stop or be stopped.

Help everyone
be 'good' gossips

You only want to tell opinion formers about your idea once but for general tabloid readers and soap fans, tell them as many times as you can.

How many times a day do you read, hear or watch the same news story from different sources? Lots.

But you are the only person telling everyone about your idea, so you've got to tell them lots of times yourself. If they are not interested they are deaf to it, so keep telling them.

One day they will hear it, but maybe not from you. It could be from a friend or colleague or online, from someone they trust. But once that happens they will love hearing it from you, as it is reinforcing the fact that they are right to be engaged.

Then they will tell everyone they know.

The Alchemist Espresso Bar in Brighton, England.
It's an actual quote as well (I checked!)

179

Help journalists
show off

Don't try to get journalists to simply write about your idea. Get them to be part of the story. Help them use it to show how good they are or to show off about their part in your success.

While promoting the school reunion website Friends Reunited, we invited journalists to write a story about their own old school friends who we would help find for them. This enabled them to go back to their school and show off to their old school mates under the premise that they were writing a newspaper feature. "What do you do? Work in a local bank or a shop? Really? I'm a writer for a popular newspaper in London..." We achieved endless amounts of coverage from journalists showing off.

As many freelance journalists work in coffee shops, I'm hoping the same idea may work for this book!

Help celebrities
feel loved

Yes, the public still love celebrities, which is why they listen to what they say.

Major UK radio and TV presenter Chris Moyles helped raise money for Comic Relief by climbing Kilimanjaro. He is a well-known tweeter but he didn't take his phone for the climb. So he didn't tweet – yet his Twitter following grew by 20,000. Meanwhile our official (but not famous) tweeter tweeted the climb live. In terms of followers, our official Twitter account grew by only a quarter of his!

Celebrity is a competitive world, though, and as new ones reach the front page A-list, others drift out of the news. You need to show celebrities how they will be more loved if they talk about your idea. If they believe you, they will back you.

So sit back and relax for a moment, with the guilty pleasure of flicking through celeb-filled gossip mags to make sure you are up-to-date with who is on the A-list and who has fallen down to D. Then approach the ones with the most relevant fans for your idea and show them how they will appear cooler or more caring, sporty or intellectual, if they talk about it.

(11) work where you like
Join the movement

Uncle Merv's in Johannesburg. The coolest coffee shop in the world.

You are in the right place

Do you look at people who are changing their lives and the world around you and think, I can do that, I could have come up with that idea?

You can. They are the same as you and I. Many of them can't believe their luck. Many of them work out of coffee shops, hubs and home and so don't see their success as a result of their hard work, channelled in the right way to the right people.

They see it that they just happened to be in the right place at the right time.

Now is the right time

"*Unfinished is exciting. We all die unfinished.*"

Simon Stephens, dramatist

At the top of a ladder you might gain more money.
During a journey you will gain memories to treasure.

www.WorkWhereYouLike.com

Join the movement

- Share tips and stories with the community
- More success stories and bonus chapters
- Apps and technology to use
- Inspiring news, blogs, websites and publications
- The best coffee shops from around the world

mymq gjfznzbrshhrtsohmnnb
VODAFONE 11175107

Not every coffee shop makes it as easy as you'd hope. The longest Wi-Fi code in the world ever in La Rosa dei Venti, Venice – and I never managed to make it work.

To Helen, Molly, Bob, Rose and Audrey. This book is for you. It's why I am who I am. I apologise for the downsides and hope you are inspired by the upsides.

Special thanks to:
Greg and Janine Cook, Rupert Edwards, Alan Long, Lucy Baker, Shane Parrish, Sandi Friend, Chris Campbell, Cate Ferguson, Hannah & Sacha and my friends and fellow coffee drinkers around the Artisan Coffee Shop neighbourhood in West London for all your inspiration and enthusiastic responses to my numerous requests for help.

Best of Smart Thinking

This book is on this shelf because of the great work of the following people. Please support them.

Smart reading for your library

It's Not How Good You Are, It's How Good You Want To Be
Paul Arden
www.paularden.com

What's Mine Is Yours
Rachel Botsman & Roo Rogers
www.rachelbotsman.com

Happier: Can you learn to be happy?
Tal Ben-Shahar
www.talbenshahar.com

Flow: The classic work on how to achieve happiness
Mihaly Csikszentmihalyi
www.cgu.edu/pages/4751.asp

Outliers: The Story of Success
Malcolm Gladwell
www.gladwell.com

What Would Google Do?
Jeff Jarvis
www.buzzmachine.com

The Lean Startup
Eric Ries
www.theleanstartup.com

The 4-Hour Workweek
Timothy Ferriss
www.fourhourworkweek.com

A technique for producing ideas
James Webb Young
McGraw-Hill Advertising Classic

Antifragile
Nassim Nicholas Taleb
www.fooledbyrandomness.com

Screw Business As Usual
Richard Branson
www.virginunite.screwbusinessasusual.com

The Continuum Concept: In Search of Happiness Lost
Jean Liedloff
www.continuum-concept.org

Photographers to work with.

I took most photos in the book on my iPhone but the good ones were taken by great photographers! Please consider working with them.

P 11, 18, 22, 26, 53, 58, 89, 130, 159, 161, 167, 170, 173
          Sandi Friend - www.sandifriend.co.uk

P6   Micha Theiner - www.michatheiner.com
P93   Giulia Mulè - www.mondomulia.com
P80   Jeff Moore - www.jeffmoorephoto.co.uk
P82   Mark Hakansson - www.hakansson.co.uk
P112,132 Gareth Davies - www.gdaviesphoto.com
P70   Mari Sheibley for Foursquare - www.marisheibley.com
P60   JP Masclet - www.jpmasclet.com

And courtesy of the following

P14, 100 Fernandez & Wells
P84   Starbucks
P110   David Pearl
P112   Square Mile Coffee
P148   Caffé Nero
P157   Artisan Coffee

Great magazines mentioned in the book.
Pick up in a newsagent or contact them to subscribe.

Fast Company	-	www.fastcompany.com
Flow	-	www.flowmagazine.com
Frankie	-	www.frankie.com.au
Monitor	-	www.monitor-magazine.com
Smith Journal	-	www.smithjournal.com.au
Wired	-	www.wired.com

Where to read more
from the cuttings and quotes

P8 quote
Crosscut
http://bit.ly/1OgrTkr

P18 cutting
Selwyn Parker
Business Destinations
http://bit.ly/YL7ZO9
published by World News Media
© World News Media

P22 cutting
Margarette Driscoll
The Sunday Times
http://thetim.es/z5CIXc

P23 quote
www.grahamjones.co.uk

P27 quote
http://www.sadiqkhan.co.uk
The Guardian
www.guardian.co.uk

P27 quote
Stanley McChrystal
http://bit.ly/1OifD2U
Fast Company
www.fastcompany.com

P35 tweet
Mike Mathieson, CEO, Cake
www.cakegroup.com

P37 quote
Richard Branson, Founder Virgin Group
http://bit.ly/13lpX69

P40, 41 T-shirt
Howies
www.howies.co.uk

P33 cutting
PR Week
www.prweek.com/uk

P89 cutting
Josh Fanning
supplement in Collect magazine
www.collectmag.com.au

P92 quote
Tony Hsieh, CEO Zappos
www.zappos.com
Fast Company

P99 quote
Alain du Botton
www.alaindebotton.com

P97 Survey
YouGov
www.yougov.co.uk

P98 quote
Jack Dorsey, Founder of Twitter &
Square.
www.twitter.com/jack

P108 Poster
WorkSnug / Plantronics
www.worksnug.com

P115 quote
Alvin Toffler
www.alvintoffler.net

P130 Cutting
Margarette Driscoll
Sunday Times
http://thetim.es/z5CIXc

P137 Tweet
Graham Linehan
www.twitter.com/Glinner

P141 quote
Biz Stone, Co-Founder of Twitter
www.twitter.com

P141 quote
Loic Le Meur
www.leweb.co

P162 quote
Marc Andreessen.
www.blog.pmarca.com

P169 quote
Steve Yankovich, VP, Ebay mobile
www.ebay.co.uk

P162 quote
Robert Kyncl
www.youtube.com

P184 quote
Simon Stephens
https://twitter.com/StephensSimon
from The Guardian www.guardian.co.uk

P22 cutting
Phil Daoust
The Guardian
http://bit.ly/XUyUqF

Continue following the 'Out of Office' success stories

J.K. Rowling	-	www.jkrowling.com
Richard Tait	-	www.boomboombrands.com
Craig Newmark	-	www.craigslist.org
Michael Acton Smith	-	www.moshimonsters.com
Jamie Coomarasamy	-	www.bbc.co.uk/worldserviceradio
Dennis Crowley	-	www.foursquare.com
Tom Watson	-	www.tom-watson.co.uk
Lizzie Bain	-	www.ozonecoffee.co.uk
Andrew Brackin	-	www.tomorrowsweb.co.uk
Mark Dixon	-	www.regus.co.uk

Published in 2013 by
Blue Dot World Ltd
105 Wendell Road
London W12 9SD

Contact the publisher for all requests
helen@bluedotworld.com
www.bluedotagency.com

Designed by Sane & Able
www.saneandable.co.uk

Cover design by Shane Parrish
www.parrishnyc.com

Printed by Empress Litho Limited
On paper produced by sustainably managed forests

ISBN 978-0-9576123-0-3

All information was accurate at time of going to press

Any inadvertent omissions can be rectified in future editions

A catalogue record of this book is available from the British Library

GET BY
in GERMAN

ULI BONK
ROBERT TILLEY

LANGUAGE CONSULTANT
SABINE ASENKERSCHBAUMER

Published by BBC Active, an imprint of Educational Publishers LLP, part of the
Pearson Education Group, Edinburgh Gate, Harlow, Essex CM20 2JE, England

© Educational Publishers LLP 2007

BBC logo © BBC 1996. BBC and BBC ACTIVE are trademarks of the British Broadcasting
Corporation

First published 1998. This edition published 2007.
Reprinted 2007, 2008.

ISBN: 978-1-4066-1163-9

Cover design: Emma Wallace
Cover photograph: Westend61/Punchstock
Insides concept design: Nicolle Thomas
Layout: eMC Design (www.emcdesign.org.uk)
Commissioning editor: Debbie Marshall
Project editor: Melanie Kramers
Project assistant: Hannah Beatson
Senior production controller: Man Fai Lau
Marketing: Fiona Griffiths, Paul East

Audio producer for the new edition: Martin Williamson, Prolingua Productions
Sound engineer: Dave Morritt, at Studio AVP
Presenters: Gertrude Thoma, Peter Stark, William Ludwig, DeNica Fairman,
Bill Dufris, Jane Whittenshaw
Original audio producer: John Green, tefl tapes
Original sound engineer and music: Tim Woolf

Printed and bound in China (CTPSC/06).
The Publisher's policy is to use paper manufactured from sustainable forests.

All photographs supplied by Alamy Images.
p9 Lightworks Media; p11 f1 online; p14 vario images GmbH & Co.KG; p16 Arco Images;
p18 mediacolor's; p23 Iain Masterton; p26 Mike Booth; p30 David R. Frazier Photolibrary,
Inc.; p31 Leslie Garland Picture Library; p33 BennettPhoto; p40 nagelestock.com;
p42 imagebroker; p45 Arcaid; p46 David Crausby; p49 archivberlin Fotoagentur GmbH;
p57 INTERFOTO Pressebildagentur; p60 Yadid Levy; p61 Danita Delimont; p62 Yadid
Levy; p64 Joern Sackermann; p66 Iain Masterton; p72 Jon Arnold Images; p75 Iain
Masterton; p77 Yadid Levy; p83 imagebroker; p84 DEPLiX; p87 Simon Reddy; p94 Simon
Reddy; p97 foodfolio; p100 FAN travelstock; p102 UKraft; p107 FAN travelstock;
p108 Jochen Tack; p111 Joern Sackermann; p115 Michael Klinec; p119 vario images
GmbH & Co.KG; p124 David R. Frazier Photolibrary, Inc.; p128 David Sanger
Photography.

Contents

How to **use this book**

Get By in German is divided into colour-coded topics to help you find what you need quickly. Each unit contains practical travel tips to help you get around and understand the country, and a phrasemaker, to help you say what you need to and understand what you hear.

As well as listing key phrases, **Get By in German** aims to help you understand how the language works so that you can build your own phrases and start to communicate independently. The check out dialogues within each section show the language in action, and the try it out activities give you an opportunity to practise for yourself. The link up sections pick out the key structures and give helpful notes about their use. A round-up of all the basic grammar can be found in the Language Builder, pp131-137.

In German, all nouns (things, people, concepts) are either masculine, feminine or neuter, and this affects other words related to them, such as the words for 'the' and 'a'. There are also often masculine and feminine versions of people's occupations, jobs and nationalities, shown in this book as, for example, Student/Studentin, meaning a male student/female student.

If you've bought the pack with the audio CD, you'll be able to listen to a selection of the most important phrases and check out dialogues, as well as all the as if you were there activities. You can use the book on its own, but the CD will help you to improve your pronunciation.

sounds German

German words are usually pronounced exactly the way they are written, and you usually pronounce every letter, including the final **-e** (pronounced rather like an English 'uh'). This book uses a pronunciation guide, based on English sounds, to help you start speaking German.

stress

Long words in German are often a combination of several shorter words, so it may help with pronunciation to split the long word into its individual parts. In this book a stressed syllable is shown in the pronunciation guide by bold:

danke *danke*   kilometer *keelomayter*

vowels

	sounds like ...	shown as ...
a	'a' in 'cat'	a
	or 'a' in 'car'	aa
ai and **ay**	'i' in 'pile'	iy
au	'ow' in 'cow'	ow
ä	'e' in 'let'	e
	or 'ay' in 'pay'	ay
äu	'oy' in 'boy'	oy
e	'e' in 'let'	e
	or 'ay' in 'pay'	ay
ei and **ey**	'i' in 'pile'	iy
eu	'oy' in 'boy'	oy
i	'i' in 'hit'	i
	or 'ee' in 'meet'	ee
ie	'ee' in 'meet'	ee
o	'o' in 'lot'	o
	or 'o' in 'bone'	oh
ö	'er' in 'fern'	er
u	'oo' in 'book'	oo
	or 'oo' in 'room'	ooh
ü	'ew' in 'dew'	ew
y	'ew' in 'dew'	ew
	or 'ee' in 'meet'	ee

consonants

Many German consonants are pronounced in a similar way to English. All doubled consonants are pronounced with an extra long sound.

	sounds like ...	shown as ...
b	'b' in 'but'	b
	or 'p' in 'pencil'	p
c	'k' in 'kit'	k
ch	somewhere between the 'ch' in 'loch' and 'k' in 'kit'	k
	or 'sh' in 'shut'	sh
d	'd' in 'dog'	d
	or 't' in 'tin'	t

f	'f' in 'feet'	f
g	'g' in 'got'	g
	or 'k' in 'kit'	k
h	'h' in 'hard'	h
j	'y' in 'you'	y
l	'l' in 'look'	l
m	'm' in 'mat'	m
n	'n' in 'not'	n
p	'p' in 'pack'	p
qu	'k+v'	kv
r	roll at the back of the mouth	r
s	's' in 'set'	s
	or 'z' in 'zoo'	z
	or 'sh' in 'shut'	sh
sch	'sh' in 'shut'	sh
ß	'ss' in 'stress'	ss
t	't' in 'tin'	t
v	'f' in 'feet'	f
	or sometimes 'v' in 'voice'	v
w	'v' in 'voice'	v
x	'x' in 'taxi'	ks
z	'ts' in 'hits'	ts

alphabet

Here's a guide to how the letters of the German alphabet are pronounced, which may be useful for spelling your name or an address. The umlaut means that there are three extra vowels in German: **ä** ('a' umlaut), **ö** ('o' umlaut) and **ü** ('u' umlaut). The **ß** symbol represents a double 'ss' and is called 's z' or 'scharfes s'.

A *aa*	**Ä** *ay*	**B** *bay*	**C** *tsay*	**D** *day*	**E** *ay*
F *ef*	**G** *gay*	**H** *haa*	**I** *ee*	**J** *yot*	**K** *kaa*
L *el*	**M** *em*	**N** *en*	**O** *oh*	**Ö** *er*	**P** *pay*
Q *koo*	**R** *ayr*	**S** *es*	**ß** *es tset/ sharfes es*	**T** *tay*	**U** *oo*
Ü *ew*	**V** *fow*	**W** *vay*	**X** *iks*	**Y** *ewpsilon*	**Z** *tset*

Bare **Necessities**

phrasemaker

greetings
you may say ...

Hello!	Hallo!	*hallo*
Good day!	Guten Tag!	*goohten taak*
Good morning!	Guten Morgen!	*goohten morgen*
Good evening!	Guten Abend!	*goohten aabent*
Goodbye!	Auf Wiedersehen! (formal)	*owf veederzayen*
	Tschüss! (informal)	*tshewss*
See you ...	Bis ...	*bis*
soon.	bald.	*balt*
tomorrow.	morgen.	*morgen*
Nice to meet you!	Angenehm! (formal)	*angenaym*
	Freut mich! (less formal)	*froyt mish*
How are you?	Wie geht's? (informal)/	*vee gayts*
	Wie geht es Ihnen? (formal)	*vee gayt es eenen*
Good, thank you.	Gut, danke.	*gooht danke*
May I introduce Mr/ Mrs/Ms ...	Darf ich vorstellen? Herr/Frau ...	*daarf ish fohrshtellen herr/frow*

other useful phrases

you may say …

yes/no	ja/nein	*yaa/niyn*
please	bitte	*bitte*
thank you very much	vielen Dank/danke schön	*feelen dank/danke shern*
of course	natürlich/ selbstverständlich	*natewrlish/ zelpstfershtendlish*
You're welcome.	Bitte schön. Keine Ursache.	*bitte shern kiyne oohrzake*
Excuse me./Sorry.	Entschuldigung.	*entshooldeegoong*
I'm sorry.	Tut mir Leid/ Entschuldigung.	*tooht meer liyt/ entshooldeegoong*
Excuse me?	Wie bitte?	*vee bitte*
Here you are.	Bitte schön.	*bitte shern*
It's very … nice. interesting.	Es ist sehr … schön. interessant.	*es ist zayr shern interessant*

where is/are …?

you may say …

Excuse me, where is … the station? the town centre? Charlotten Street?	Entschuldigung, wo ist … der Bahnhof? das Zentrum? die Charlottenstraße?	*entshooldigoong voh ist der baanhohf das tsentroom dee charlottenshtraasse*
Is/Are there … here? a chemist's a lift a bus any toilets	Gibt es hier … eine Apotheke? einen Fahrstuhl? einen Bus? Toiletten?	*geept es heer iyne apotayke iynen faarshtoohl iynen boos toletetten*

Bare **Necessities**

you may hear ...

rechts/links/ geradeaus	*reshts/links/ geraadeows*	right/left/straight ahead
Das ist hier/dort.	*das ist heer/dort*	That is here/there.
Wohin möchten Sie?	*vohhin mershten zee*	Where would you like to go?
Tut mir Leid, ich weiß es nicht.	*tooht meer liyt ish viyss es nisht*	I'm sorry, I don't know.

check out 1

You ask a passer-by for directions.

○ Entschuldigung, gibt es hier einen Bus?
*entshooldigoong geept es heer **iy**nen boos*

- Wohin möchten Sie?
vohhin mershten zee

○ Zum Bahnhof, bitte.
*tsoom **baan**hohf **bi**tte*

- Geradeaus.
*geraade**ows***

○ Vielen Dank.
feelen dank

Q Where do you want to go?
Where can you find a bus?

do you have …?

What is that called?	Wie heißt das?	*vee hiysst das*
Do you have …	Haben Sie …	*haaben zee*
a table?	einen Tisch?	*iynen tish*
a double room?	ein Doppelzimmer?	*iyn doppeltsimmer*
any batteries?	Batterien?	*battereeyen*
any toothpaste?	Zahnpasta?	*tsaanpasta*

I'd like …

I'd like …	Ich möchte …	*ish mershte*
a ticket.	eine Karte.	*iyne karte*
a CD.	eine CD.	*iyne tsayday*
a kilo of apples.	ein Kilo Äpfel.	*iyn keelo epfel*
How much is it?	Was kostet das?	*vas kostet das*

getting things straight

I don't understand!	Ich verstehe nicht!	*ish fershtaye nisht*
I only speak a little German.	Ich spreche nur ein bisschen Deutsch.	*ish shpreshe noohr iyn bissshen doytsh*
Once again, please.	Noch einmal, bitte.	*nok iynmaal, bitte*
Slowly, please.	Langsam, bitte.	*langzaam bitte*
Do you speak English?	Sprechen Sie Englisch?	*shpreshen zee english*
Please spell it.	Bitte buchstabieren Sie.	*bitte boohkshtabeeren zee*
Please write it down.	Bitte schreiben Sie es auf.	*bitte shriyben zee es owf*
What does … mean?	Was bedeutet …?	*vas bedoytet*
I don't know.	Ich weiß nicht.	*ish viyss nisht*

check out 2

○ Wie bitte? Ich verstehe nicht.
vee bitte. ish fershtaye nisht

- Wurst mit Salat.
voorst mit zalaat

○ Ich spreche nur ein bisschen Deutsch. Sprechen Sie Englisch?
ish shpreshe noohr iyn bissshen doytsh. shpreshen zee english

- Natürlich. Sausage with salad.
natewrlish

Q What do you ask the waiter?

talking about yourself

you may say ...

My name is ...	Ich heiße .../	*ish hiysse/*
	Mein Name ist ...	*miyn naame ist*
I'm from ...	Ich komme aus ...	*ish komme ows*
Scotland.	Schottland.	*schottlant*
(See nationalities, p18)		
I'm on holiday.	Ich mache Urlaub.	*ish maake oohrlowp*
I'm on a business trip.	Ich bin auf Geschäftsreise.	*ish bin owf gesheftsriyze*
I have ... children.	Ich habe ... Kinder.	*ish haabe ... kinder*
two	zwei	*tsviy*
no	keine	*kiyne*
I am ... years old.	Ich bin ... Jahre alt.	*ish bin ... yaare alt*
I am ...	Ich bin ...	*ish bin*
single.	single.	*singl*
married.	verheiratet.	*ferhiyraatet*
separated.	getrennt.	*getrennt*
divorced.	geschieden.	*gesheeden*
I have ...	Ich habe ...	*ish haabe*
a boyfriend.	einen Freund.	*iynen froynt*
a girlfriend.	eine Freundin.	*iyne froyndin*
a partner.	einen Partner/eine Partnerin.	*iynen partner/iyne partnerin*
I am ...	Ich bin ...	*ish bin*
a web designer.	Webdesigner/ Webdesignerin.	*vepdeziyner/ vepdeziynerin*
a doctor.	Arzt/Ärztin.	*artst/ayrtstin*
a student.	Student/Studentin.	*shtoodent/ shtoodentin*
I work in ...	Ich arbeite in ...	*ish aarbiyte in*
a shop.	einem Geschäft.	*iynem gesheft*
an office.	einem Büro.	*iynem bewro*

Bare **Necessities**

you may hear ...

Wie heißen Sie? (formal)	*vee hiyssen zee*	What is your name?
Wie heißt du? (informal)	*vee hiyst doo*	
Woher kommen Sie? (formal)	*vohhayr kommen zee*	Where are you from?
Machen Sie hier Urlaub?	*maken zee heer oohrlowp*	Are you on holiday?
Wie gefällt es Ihnen?	*vee gefellt es eenen*	How do you like it?
Was sind Sie von Beruf?	*vas zint zee fon beroohf*	What do you do?
Sind Sie verheiratet?	*zint zee ferhiyraatet*	Are you married?
Haben Sie Kinder?	*haaben zee kinder*	Do you have children?
Wie alt sind Sie?	*vee alt zint zee*	How old are you?

check out 3

You're staying in a hotel in Berlin, and get chatting to another guest.

○ Guten Tag.
goohten taag

- Machen Sie hier Urlaub?
maken zee heer oohrlowp

○ Nein, ich bin auf Geschäftsreise.
niyn ish bin owf gesheftsriyze

- Wie gefällt es Ihnen?
vee gefellt es eenen

○ Es ist sehr interessant.
es ist zayr interessant

Q Are you in Berlin on holiday or business?
What do you think of the city?

changing money

you may say ...

I'd like to ...	Ich möchte ...	*ish* **mersh**te
change some money.	Geld tauschen.	*gelt* **tow**shen
exchange some traveller's cheques.	Reiseschecks einlösen.	*riy*zesheks **iyn**lerzen
change £50. (See numbers, p17)	fünfzig Pfund tauschen.	**fewnf**tsig pfoont **tow**shen
What is the exchange rate today?	Wie ist der Kurs heute?	*vee ist der koors* **hoy**te
What is the pound at?	Wie steht das Pfund?	*vee shtayt das pfoont*
Do you take commission?	Nehmen Sie Kommission?	**nay**men zee kommiss**yohn**
What's the commission charge?	Wie viel ist die Kommission?	*vee feel ist dee* kommiss**yohn**

you may hear ...

Das Pfund steht bei einem Euro achtundvierzig.	*das pfoont shtayt biy iynem* **oy***ro aktoont***feert***sig*	The pound is at €1.48.
Zwei Prozent Gebühren.	*tsviy pro***tsent** *ge***bew**ren	Commission is 2%.
drei Euro fünfundvierzig	*driy* **oy**ro fewnfoont**feert**sig	€3.45

14

Bare **Necessities**

the time

What time is it?	Wie spät ist es?	*vee shpayt ist es*
What time does … start?	Wann beginnt …	*vann be**ginnt***
the performance	die Vorstellung?	*dee **fohr**shtelloong*
What time does … leave?	Wann fährt … ab?	*vann fayrt … ap*
the train	der Zug	*der tsoohk*

you may hear …

Es ist …	*es ist*	It's …
ein Uhr.	*iyn oohr*	one o'clock.
Viertel nach eins.	*feertel naak iyns*	quarter past one.
halb zwei.	*halp tsviy*	half past one.
Viertel vor zwei.	*feertel foohr tsviy*	quarter to two.
von sechs Uhr bis neun Uhr	*fon zeks oohr bis noyn oohr*	from 6 o'clock till 9 o'clock
Es beginnt/endet um …	*be**ginnt**/**en**det oom*	It starts/finishes at …
acht Uhr.	*akt oohr*	8.00.
zehn nach acht.	*tsayn nak akt*	8.10.
zehn vor neun.	*tsayn fohr noyn*	8.50.

months

January	Januar	*ya*noo-ar
February	Februar	*fay*broo-ar
March	März	*merts*
April	April	*a*pril
May	Mai	*miy*
June	Juni	*yooh*nee
July	Juli	*yooh*lee
August	August	ow*goost*
September	September	zep*tem*ber
October	Oktober	ok*toh*ber
November	November	no*vem*ber
December	Dezember	day*tsem*ber

days

Monday	Montag	*mohn*taak
Tuesday	Dienstag	*deens*taak
Wednesday	Mittwoch	*mitt*vok
Thursday	Donnerstag	*do*nnerstaak
Friday	Freitag	*friy*taak
Saturday	Samstag/Sonnabend	*zams*taag/*zonn*aabent
Sunday	Sonntag	*zonn*taak
today	heute	*hoy*te
yesterday	gestern	*ges*tern
tomorrow ...	morgen ...	*mor*gen
morning	früh	frew
afternoon	Nachmittag	*nak*mittaak
next week	nächste Woche	*nayk*ste *vo*ke
late morning/lunch time	Vormittag/Mittag	*fohr*mittaak/*mit*taak
this evening/tonight	heute Abend	*hoy*te *aa*bent

Bare **Necessities**

numbers

0	null	*nooll*		22	zweiund-zwanzig	*tsviyoonttsvantsig*
1	eins	*iyns*		23	dreiundzwanzig	*driyoonttsvantsig*
2	zwei	*tsviy*		30	dreißig	*driyssig*
3	drei	*driy*		40	vierzig	*feertsig*
4	vier	*feer*		50	fünfzig	*fewnftsig*
5	fünf	*fewnf*		51	einundfünfzig	*iynoontfewnftsig*
6	sechs	*zeks*		60	sechzig	*zeshtsig*
7	sieben	*zeeben*		62	zweiundsechzig	*tsviyoontzeshtsig*
8	acht	*akt*		70	siebzig	*zeeptsig*
9	neun	*noyn*		73	dreiundsiebzig	*driyoontzeepsig*
10	zehn	*tsayn*		80	achtzig	*akttsig*
11	elf	*elf*		90	neunzig	*noyntsig*
12	zwölf	*tsverlf*		100	(ein)hundert	*(iyn)hoondert*
13	dreizehn	*driytsayn*		103	(ein)hundertdrei	*(iyn)hoondertdriy*
14	vierzehn	*feertsayn*		200	zweihundert	*tsviyhoondert*
15	fünfzehn	*fewnftsayn*		315	dreihundertfün-	*driyhoondert-*
16	sechzehn	*zeshtsayn*			fzehn	*fewnftsayn*
17	siebzehn	*zeeptsayn*		825	achthundert-	*akthoondertfewnf-*
18	achtzehn	*akttsayn*			fünfundzwanzig	*oonttsvansig*
19	neunzehn	*noyntsayn*		1000	(ein)tausand/ein	*(iyn)towsant*
20	zwanzig	*tsvantsig*			Tausand	
21	einund-	*iynoont-*		1590	(ein)tausandfünf-	*(iyn)towsantfewnf-*
	zwanzig	*tsvantsig*			hundertneunzig	*hoondertnoynsig*

ordinals

1st	erste(r)	*erste(r)*
2nd	zweite(r)	*tsviyte(r)*
3rd	dritte(r)	*dritte(r)*
10th	zehnte(r)	*tsaynte(r)*
15th	fünfzehnte(r)	*fewnftsaynte(r)*
20th	zwanzigste(r)	*tsvantsigste(r)*
30th	dreißigste(r)	*driyssigste(r)*

countries & nationalities

Australia: Australian	Australien: Australier(in)	*owstraalyen: owstraalyer(in)*
Austria: Austrian	Österreich: Österreicher(in)	*ersterriysh: ersterriysher(in)*
Canada: Canadian	Kanada: Kanadier(in)	*kanada: kanaadyer(in)*
England: English	England: Engländer(in)	*englant: englender(in)*
Germany: German	Deutschland: Deutscher/Deutsche	*doytshlant: doytsher/doytshe*
Great Britain: British	Großbritannien: Brite/Britin	*grohssbritaanyen: brite/britin*
Ireland: Irish	Irland: Ire/Irin	*irlant: eere/eerin*
New Zealand: New Zealander	Neuseeland: Neuseeländer(in)	*noyzaylant: noyzaylender(in)*
Northern Ireland: Northern Irish	Nordirland: Nordire/Nordirin	*nortirlant: norteere/norteerin*
Scotland: Scottish	Schottland: Schotte/Schottin	*shottlant: shotte/shottin*
South Africa: South African	Südafrika: Südafrikaner(in)	*sewtafrika: sewtafrikaaner(in)*
Switzerland: Swiss	Schweiz: Schweizer(in)	*shviyts/shviytser(in)*
United States: American	Vereinigte Staaten: Amerikaner(in)	*feriynigte shtaaten: amerikaaner(in)*
Wales: Welsh	Wales: Waliser(in)	*vayls: valeezer(in)*

Bare **Necessities**

sound check

z is a very sharp sound in German, pronounced like the 'ts' in 'hits'.

Zahnpasta *tsaanpasta*   zehn *tsayn*

You'll often see it in the combination 'tz':

Platz *plats*   Mütze *mewtse*

try it out

lucky numbers
Who has got lottery numbers a, b and c?

a   siebzehn dreizehn zwölf
b   fünfzig elf dreiundvierzig
c   sechzehn dreizehn null drei

Claudia Hauswirt 16 13 03   Ruth Städing 17 13 12
Christel Ahlf 06 51 95   Volker Bruns 16 73 12
Peter Wiese 50 11 43   Britta Nessel 81 20 65

as if you were there
You're on holiday in Germany, and get chatting to a man at a bar. Follow the prompts to play your part.

Guten Abend. Wie geht es Ihnen?
(Say Good evening. Then say you're fine, thanks)
Ich bin Peter. Wie heißen Sie?
(Say your name is Sarah)
Woher kommen Sie?
(Say you're English, and you come from Manchester)

linkup

listening & replying

When people ask you questions about yourself, such as:

Haben Sie Kinder? Do you have children?

it's tempting to reply using the same form of the verb haben (have), but instead you need to change haben to ich habe (I have) in the reply:

Ja, ich **habe** Kinder./Nein, **ich habe keine** Kinder. Yes, I have children./No, I don't have children.

Some other common questions and possible replies:

Woher kommen Sie? – Ich komme aus Berlin. Where do you come from? – I come from Berlin.

Wie heißen Sie? – Ich heiße Peter. What is your name? – My name is Peter.

If you're using ich, verbs generally end in -e, and if you're using Sie verbs generally end in -en.

Ich komm**e**	Sie komm**en**
Ich heiß**e**	Sie heiß**en**
Ich hab**e**	Sie hab**en**

For more on verb endings see the Language Builder, pp133-134. ⋯⋯⋗

the way you say things

You can't always translate things word for word from one language to another.

Tut mir Leid (I'm sorry) literally means '(It) does me sorrow', and Wie geht's? (How are you?) is literally 'How does it go?'.

So sometimes it is worth learning the whole phrase rather than the individual words.

Getting **Around**

by air

Air travel can work out cheaper than train, especially over long distances. The main national airlines are Lufthansa, Deutsche BA, LTU and Germanwings, the country's first low-cost airline.

by bus

The nearest Germany has to a national bus network are the **Deutsche Touring** tourist services. Long-distance buses cover some of Germany's most popular tourist routes, such as the **Romantische Straße** (Romantic Road). Daily bus services also connect Berlin with most major cities. See schedules and fares at: **www.deutsche-touring.de**. Most country districts have local buses, but they can be irregular.

by boat

Regular boat services travel the Rhine and other rivers such as the Danube, Elbe, Main and Moselle. The main operator is the KD company: **www.k-d.com**. Deutsche Bahn (German Railways) operate ferry services on the **Bodensee** (Lake Constance), and the larger lakes all have privately-run pleasure boat services.

by car

Germany's **Autobahnen** (motorways) are legendary, and justifiably so. The country is covered by a comprehensive network totalling thousands of miles. There are no tolls, but they can be very crowded. Service stations are found every 30 miles or so, but petrol prices there tend to be considerably more expensive than at off-motorway sites. Germany's main automobile club, the ADAC, comes to the assistance of motorists in need of breakdown help, charging only the cost of repairs, parts or towing. Emergency telephones are positioned at one-and-a-half-mile intervals.

car hire

All major international car hire firms have offices at airports and city train stations – look for the **Autovermietung** signs. Hire charges start at around €40 per day. A national driving licence and passport are the only documents required, and credit cards are the preferred method of payment.

train travel

The privatized **Deutsche Bahn** (German Railways) is a model rail service. Their country-wide network serves even the smallest communities, while the ultra high-speed InterCity Express (ICE) is faster than air travel on some routes (Munich–Frankfurt, for instance). Other options are the InterCity (slower and cheaper than the InterCity Express), the EuroCity (connecting German cities with destinations abroad), the InterRegio (for national travel), the InterRegioExpress and the RegionalExpress (connecting towns within specific regions), the Regionalbahn (slow regional trains calling at every stop) and the City Night Line, an extremely comfortable hotel-on-wheels.

The Deutsche Bahn has a wide range of special ticket offers, which changes with confusing frequency. The all-time favourite is the German Rail Pass, available for periods of four to ten days, which also allows travel on certain ferries. You can check train information, fares and special offers at **www.bahn.de**.

phrasemaker

finding the way

Excuse me ...	Entschuldigung ...	*entshooldigoong*
Where is ... please?	Wo ist ... bitte?	*voh ist ... bitte*
the station	der Bahnhof	*der baanhohf*
the bus station	der Busbahnhof	*der boosbaanhohf*
the bus stop	die Bushaltestelle	*dee booshalteshtelle*
Is there ... here?	Gibt es hier ...	*geept es heer*
a chemist's	eine Apotheke?	*iyne apotayke*
an internet café	ein Internetcafé?	*iyn internetkaffay*
a cash machine	einen Geldautomat?	*iynen geltowtomaat*
Are there any ... near here?	Gibt es hier in der Nähe ...	*geept es heer in der naye*
toilets	Toiletten?	*toaletten*
shops	Geschäfte?	*geshefte*
How far is ...	Wie weit ist ...	*vee viyt ist*
the bank?	die Bank?	*dee bank*
the hotel?	das Hotel?	*das hotel*
the airport?	der Flughafen?	*der flookhaafen*
I'm looking for the tourist information office.	Ich suche die Touristeninformation.	*ish zoohke dee tooristeninformatsyohn*
Is ... far from here?	Ist ... weit von hier?	*ist ... viyt fon heer*
the cathedral	die Kathedrale	*dee katedraale*
the city centre	die Innenstadt	*dee innenshtat*
the old part of town	die Altstadt	*dee altshtat*
Is this the right way to the ...	Ist dies der Weg zum ...	*ist deez der vayg tsoom*
town centre?	Stadtzentrum?	*shtattsentroom*
market square?	Marktplatz?	*marktplats*
port?	Hafen?	*haafen*
airport?	Flughafen?	*flookhaafen*

(For a list of shops see p60, and for places to visit see p101.)

Getting **Around**

you may hear ...

rechts/links/ geradeaus	*reshts/links/ geraadeows*	right/left/ straight on
auf der ... Seite	*owf der ... ziyte*	on the ...
rechten	*reshten*	right
linken	*linken*	left
... Ecke	*... eke*	... corner
an der	*an der*	at the
um die	*oom dee*	around the
Sie ...	*zee*	you ...
gehen	*gayen*	go
fahren	*faaren*	drive
die ... Straße	*dee ... shtraasse*	the ... street
nächste	*nekste*	next
erste	*erste*	first
zweite	*tsviyte*	second
ungefähr ...	*oongefayr*	about ...
zweihundert Meter/ Kilometer	*tsviyhoondert mayter/ keelomayter*	200 metres/ kilometres
am Ende der Straße	*am ende der shtraasse*	at the end of the street
hier/da	*heer/daa*	here/there
bis	*bis*	as far as
über ...	*ewber*	across ...
die Brücke	*dee brewke*	the bridge
den Platz	*dayn plats*	the square
Es ist ziemlich ...	*es ist tseemlish*	It is fairly ...
weit.	*viyt*	far.
nah.	*naa*	close.
bei	*biy*	near
gegenüber	*gaygenewber*	opposite
hinter	*hinter*	behind
vor	*fohr*	in front of
neben	*nayben*	next to

check out 1

You stop a passer-by to ask the way to the museum.

○ Entschuldigung, wo ist das Museum, bitte?
*ent**shool**digoong voh ist das moo**zay**oom **bi**tte*

- Das Museum? Das ist die nächste Straße links.
*das moo**zay**oom. das ist dee **nek**ste **shtraa**sse links*

○ Wie weit ist das, bitte?
*vee viyt ist das **bi**tte*

- Ungefähr fünfhundert Meter.
*oonge**fayr fewnf**hoondert **may**ter*

○ Vielen Dank.
*fee**len dank*

Q Is the museum on the left or on the right?
How far away is it?

Getting **Around**

pedestrian signs
you may see ...

Kreuzung	crossing
Fußgängerzone	pedestrian zone
Fahrradweg	cycle path

hiring a car or motorbike
you may say ...

I'd like to hire ... please.	Ich möchte bitte ...	*ish mershte bitte*
a car	ein Auto mieten.	*iyn owto meeten*
a motorbike	ein Motorrad mieten.	*iyn motohrraat meeten*
a bike	ein Fahrrad leihen.	*iyn faahraat liyen*
for ...	für ...	*fewr*
three days	drei Tage	*driy taage*
one week	eine Woche	*iyne voke*
How much is it per ...	Was kostet das pro ...	*vas kostet das proh*
day?	Tag?	*taak*
week?	Woche?	*voke*
Is insurance included?	Versicherung inklusive?	*ferzisheroong inkloozeeve*
small/fairly large	klein/ziemlich groß	*kliyn/tseemlish grohss*

you may hear ...

Ihren Führerschein, bitte.	*eeren fewrershiyn bitte*	Your driving licence, please.
Für wie lange?	*fewr vee lange*	For how long?
Das kostet fünfzig Euro pro Tag.	*das kostet fewnftsig oyro proh taak*	It costs €50 per day.

check out 2

You make enquiries about hiring a car.

- ○ Ich möchte bitte ein Auto mieten.
  ish mershte bitte iyn owto meeten

- – Selbstverständlich. Für wie lange?
  zelpstfershtendlish. fewr vee lange

- ○ Für eine Woche. Was kostet das?
  fewr iyne voke. vas kostet das

- – Das kostet zweihundert Euro pro Woche. Haben Sie Ihren Führerschein da?
  das kostet tsviyhoondert oyroh proh voke. haaben zee eeren fewrershiyn da

- ○ Natürlich, hier bitte.
  natewrlish heer bitte

  (selbstverständlich/natürlich = of course)

Q What did the salesperson ask you for?
For how long can you hire the car for €200?

at the petrol station

you may say …

Where can I find …	Wo finde ich …	*voh finde ik*
4-star?	Super?	*zoohper*
diesel?	Diesel?	*deezel*
unleaded petrol?	bleifreies Benzin?	*bliyfriyes bentseen*
self-service	selbsttanken	*zelbsttanken*
Is there a car wash here?	Gibt es hier eine Waschstraße?	*geept es heer iyne vashshtraasse*
I need some oil.	Ich brauche Öl.	*ish browke ewl*
I'd like to check my tyre pressure.	Ich möchte meinen Reifendruck prüfen.	*ish mershte miynen riyfendruck prewfen*

Getting **Around**

on the road
you may say ...

Is this the way to Berlin?	Ist dies der Weg nach Berlin?	*ist dees der vayk nak ber**leen***
How far is Hamburg?	Wie weit ist es nach Hamburg?	*vee viyt ist es nak **ham**boork*

Where is ...
  Baden-Baden?
  the motorway?
	Wo ist ...
	  Baden-Baden?
	  die Autobahn?
		voh ist
		  *baaden**baaden***
		  *dee **ow**tobaan*

Can I park here?	Kann ich hier parken?	*kann ish heer **parken***
Where is the car park?	Wo ist der Parkplatz?	*voh ist der **park**plats*

(For breakdowns see Emergencies, pp126-128.)

road signs
you may see ...

freies Parken	free parking
Parkgebühr	pay for parking
rechts halten	keep right
Vorfahrt	priority
Rastplatz	rest area
Gebühr	toll
Umleitung	diversion
Abzweigung	turn off
Sackgasse	cul-de-sac
Einbahnstraße	one way
Abfahrt/Auffahrt	motorway exit/approach

check out 3

You stop for petrol and to check the way to the motorway.

○ Guten Tag, wo finde ich bleifreies Benzin, bitte?
goohten taag vo finde ish bliyfriyes bentseen bitte

- Zapfsäule Nummer vier.
tsapfzoyle noommer feer

(you fill up)

○ Ich suche die Autobahn.
ish zoohke dee owtobaan

- Sie fahren hier die erste Straße rechts, dann geradeaus.
zee faaren heer dee erste shtraasse reshts dann geraadeows

○ Wie weit ist es nach Hannover?
vee viyt ist es nak hannohfer

- Ungefähr einhundert Kilometer.
oongefayr iynhoondert keelohmayter

Q Do you have to take the first or second street on the right?
How far is it to Hanover?

Getting **Around**

taking a taxi

you may say …

Is there a taxi rank near here?	Gibt es einen Taxi-stand in der Nähe?	*geept es **iy**nen **tak**sishtant in der **nay**e*
To this address please.	Zu dieser Adresse bitte.	*tsooh **dee**zer a**dre**sse **bi**tte*
To the Hotel Zur Post please.	Zum Hotel Zur Post bitte.	*tsoom ho**tel** tsoor post **bi**tte*
To the airport, please.	Zum Flughafen, bitte.	*tsoom **floohk**haafen, **bi**tte*
How long is it?	Wie lange dauert es?	*vee **lange dow**ert es*
How far is it?	Wie weit ist es?	*vee viyt ist es*
How much is it/will it be?	Wie viel kostet es?	*vee feel **kos**tet es*
Keep the change.	Stimmt so.	*shtimmt zoh*
This is for you.	Das ist für Sie.	*das ist fewr zee*
Can I have a receipt, please?	Kann ich bitte eine Quittung haben?	*kann ish **bi**tte **iy**ne **kvi**ttoong **haa**ben*

you may hear …

Nicht weit/lang.	*nikt viyt/lang*	Not far/long.
Es ist ganz schön weit.	*es ist gants shern viyt*	It's quite far.

public transport
you may say …

Are there … to …?	Gibt es … nach …?	*geept es … nak*
buses	Busse	*boosse*
trains	Züge	*tsewge*
trams	Straßenbahnen	*shtraassenbaanen*
Is there a shuttle service to the airport?	Gibt es einen Pendelbus zum Flughafen?	*geept es iynen pendelboos tsoom floohkhaafen*
Does this train go to the main station?	Fährt dieser Zug zum Hauptbahnhof?	*fayrt deezer tsoohk tsoom howptbaanhohf*
Which train/line goes to the town hall square?	Welcher Zug/Welche Linie fährt zum Rathausplatz?	*velsher tsoohk/velshe leenye fayrt tsoom raathowsplats*
Where is the nearest underground? tram stop?	Wo ist die nächste U-Bahn-Station? Straßenbahnhalt-estelle?	*voh ist dee naykste oohbaanshtatsyohn shtraassenbaanhalt-eshtelle*
When does the train leave?	Wann fährt der Zug ab?	*vann fayrt der tsoohk ap*
When does the train arrive?	Wann kommt der Zug an?	*vann kommt der tsoohk an*
When does the … train leave? next last	Wann geht der … Zug? nächste letzte	*vann gayt der … tsoohk nekste letste*
Where does the train to Köln leave from?	Von wo fährt der Zug nach Köln ab?	*fon voh fayrt der tsoohk nak kerln ap*
How long does the journey take?	Wie lange dauert die Fahrt?	*vee lange dowert dee faart*
Have you got a timetable?	Haben Sie einen Fahrplan?	*haaben zee iynen faarplaan*
Does this bus go to …?	Fährt dieser Bus nach …?	*fayrt deezer boos nak*
Can you tell me where to get off?	Können Sie mir sagen, wo ich aussteigen muss?	*kernnen zee meer zaagen voh ish owsshtiygen mooss*

Is there ...	Gibt es dort ...	*geept es dort*
a lift?	einen Fahrstuhl/ Aufzug?	*iynen **faar**shtoohl/ **owft**soohk*
an escalator?	eine Rolltreppe?	*iyne **roll**treppe*
a left luggage office?	eine Gepäckaufbe-wahrung?	*iyne ge**pek**owfbevaaroong*

you may hear ...

Nehmen Sie die U1.	*naymen zee dee ooh iyns*	Take the U1 line.
Gleis acht/Bahnsteig acht	*gliys akt/**baan**shtiyk akt*	platform 8
Steigen Sie in ... aus.	*shtiygen zee in ... ows*	Get off at ...
Steigen Sie in ... um.	*shtiygen zee in ... oom*	Change at ...
Ich zeige es Ihnen.	*ish **tsiy**ge es **ee**nen*	I'll show you.

U-Bhf Klosterstraße

check out 4

You want to take the train to Munich.

○ Wann fährt der Zug nach München ab?
*vann fayrt der tsoohk nak **mewn**shen ap*

- Um acht Uhr siebzehn.
*oom akt oohr **zeept**sayn*

○ Und wann kommt er in München an?
*oont vann kommt er in **mewn**shen an*

- Um zehn Uhr drei.
oom tsayn oohr driy

○ Von wo fährt der Zug ab?
fon voh fayrt der tsoohk ap

- Gleis vierzehn.
*gliys **feert**sayn*

(For more on times, see p113.)

(For more on times, see p113.)

Q What time does the train leave?
What time does it arrive?
What platform does it go from?

buying tickets
you may say …

Where is the ticket office/ticket machine, please?	Wo ist der Schalter/ der Fahrkartenauto-mat, bitte?	*voh ist der **shal**ter/ der **faar**kartenowtomaat **bit**te*
Single/Return please.	Einfach/Hin und zurück, bitte.	***iyn**fak/hin oont tsoo**rewk bit**te*
a single ticket	eine einfache Fahrkarte	*iyne **iyn**fake **faar**karte*
a return ticket	eine Rückfahrkarte	*iyne **rewk**faarkarte*
a daily travel card	eine Tageskarte	*iyne **taa**geskarte*
for two adults, one child	zwei Erwachsene, ein Kind	*tsviy er**vak**sene, iyn kint*

Getting **Around**

first/second class	erster/zweiter Klasse	*erster/**tsviy**ter **kla**sse*
today/tomorrow	heute/morgen	*hoyte/**mor**gen*
I'd like to reserve ... please.	Ich möchte ... reservieren, bitte.	*ish **mersh**te ... rezer**vee**ren, **bi**tte*
a seat	einen Platz	*iynen plats*
a couchette	einen Platz im Schlafwagen	*iynen plats im **shlaaf**vaagen*
Is there a reduction for ...	Gibt es eine Ermäßigung für ...	*geept es **iy**ne er**may**ssigoong fewr*
students?	Studenten?	*shtoo**den**ten*
senior citizens?	Rentner?	***rent**ner*
Can I buy a ticket on the bus?	Kann ich die Fahrkarte im Bus lösen?	*kann ish dee **faar**karte im boos **ler**sen*

you may hear ...

Raucher oder Nichtraucher?	*rowker ohder niktrowker*	Smoking or non-smoking?
Das kostet ... Zuschlag.	*das **kos**tet ... **tsooh**shlaak*	There is a supplement of ...
Haben sie es passend.	*haben see es **pass**ent*	You have to give the exact money.
Wann wollen Sie reisen?	*vann **vo**llen zee **riy**zen*	When do you want to travel?

check out 5

You are at the train station, buying tickets for you and your partner.

○ Guten Morgen, zwei einfache Fahrkarten nach Berlin, bitte.
goohten morgen tsviy iynfake faarkarten nak berleen bitte

- Erster oder zweiter Klasse?
erster ohder tsviyter klasse

○ Zweiter Klasse, bitte. Können wir Plätze reservieren?
tsviyter klasse bitte. kernnen veer pletse rezerveeren

- Selbstverständlich.
zelpstfershtendlish

○ Was kostet das?
vas kostet das

- Zwei einfache Fahrkarten nach Berlin: zweihundert Euro.
tsviy iynfake faarkarten nak berleen tsviyhoondert oyro

Q You are asked what day you want to travel: true or false? How much do you have to pay in total?

signs
you may see ...

Abfahrt	departures
Ankunft	arrivals
Bahnsteig/Gleis	platform
Schalter	ticket office
Wartesaal	waiting room
Schlafwagen	sleeping carriage
Auskunft/Information	information

Getting **Around**

try it out

mind the gap

Can you guess the missing words in these conversations?

1

– Entschuldigung. Was kostet eine Fahrkarte nach Köln?

○ Einfach kostet achtundsechzig Euro, hin und … kostet einhundertsechsunddreizig Euro.

– Ich möchte einen … reservieren. Und von wo fährt der Zug?

○ Von … dreizehn.

2

– … ist die Straßenbahnhaltestelle, bitte?

○ Die zweite … rechts. Ungefähr fünfzig Meter.

as if you were there

Trying to get your bearings in town, you stop a passer-by for directions. Follow the prompts to play your part.

(Say excuse me, and ask where the tourist office is)

Sie gehen hier rechts und dann die zweite links.

(Ask if it is far from here)

Nein, ungefähr zehn Minuten von hier.

(Ask if there is a bank near here)

Ja, in der Goethestraße. Die zweite Straße links.

linkup

'the' & 'a'

In German there are three different ways of saying 'the': der, die or das, because nouns (words for things, people, places etc.) can be either masculine (der Bus), feminine (die U-Bahn) or neuter (das Fahrrad).

Similarly, 'a' can be either ein or eine: ein Bus (masculine), eine U-Bahn (feminine), ein Fahrrad (neuter).

If you have more than one of something, you always use die: die Fahrräder the bicycles

The masculine word for 'the' and 'a' can change depending on how it's used in a sentence:

Ich nehme **den** Bus. I'll take the bus.
Ich möchte **einen** Kaffee, bitte. I'd like a coffee, please.

Note that nouns in German always begin with a capital letter.

For more on articles see the Language Builder, pp131-132.

Getting **around**

how to ask a question

Sometimes questions follow the same pattern as in English:

Wo ist die Bank? Where is the bank?
Ist die Kathedrale weit? Is the cathedral far?
Wie viel kostet das? How much is it?

Sometimes, however, the word order is different:

Haben Sie einen Stadtplan? Do you have a map of town?
Gibt es hier eine Apotheke? Is there a chemist near here?
Gibt es hier Toiletten? Are there any toilets here?

Note that gibt es? can mean both 'is there?' and 'are there?'.

Verbs that consist of two components, like ankommen (an and kommen) or abfahren (ab and fahren), get split up when used to ask questions. The first part of the word goes to the end of the sentence while the second part follows the question word:

Wann **kommt** der Zug **an**? When does the train arrive?
Wann **fährt** der Zug **ab**? When does the train leave?

For more handy question words see the Language Builder, p135. ·····⫶

Somewhere **to Stay**

hotels

German hotels range from the luxurious to the basic, but you can be sure that, whatever the price, they all offer clean and comfortable accommodation and efficient management. Ask at local tourist offices for listings.

All the major international chains are represented in Germany, and most allow you to book online. Look out for specialist groups, like Silence, who specialise in hotels in quiet surroundings, Gast im Schloß, who have an impressive collection of castle hotels, and the Romantik group, offering intimate stays in buildings full of character.

Before booking any city hotel, check whether a trade fair is on during your visit, as room rates can soar by as much as 50%. Most large hotels offer discounted weekend rates, so always ask whether special rates apply.

Many hotels make no charge for children sharing their parents' room on an extra bed or cot. Most major hotels have special rooms or even floors for non-smokers.

Some useful websites include:

www.germany-tourism.co.uk
www.hotel.de
www.hotellerie.de

guesthouses

Germany has no central star system for accommodation, although individual states are gradually introducing their own. This makes it difficult for the visitor to judge the difference in comfort and facilities, but usually price is the best indicator.

Pensionen are small, often privately-run hotels with a personal touch, offering meals. If this is limited to breakfast, they usually call themselves **Garni**.

Gasthäuser (singular **Gasthaus**) and **Gasthöfe** (singular **Gasthof**) are more down-to-earth establishments, often village inns with their own wine or beer **Stube** (tavern) and restaurant. They offer good (and sometimes extraordinary) value for money.

Bed & breakfast is offered in many private homes and farms in country regions. Look for signs advertising **Fremdenzimmer** (guest rooms). A green **Zimmer frei** sign means they have rooms available, while a red **Belegt** sign means there are no vacancies.

apartments

Most major cities now have a **Wohnbörse** office, where furnished houses and apartments are offered for short- and medium-term lettings.

farm holidays

The German Agricultural Association (DLG) lists more than 1,500 inspected and graded farms offering **Urlaub auf dem Bauernhof** (farm holidays). Visit **www.landtourismus.de** for full descriptions.

camping

Germany has about 2,000 officially-inspected campsites of a very high standard, many of them in areas of great natural beauty. Site fees are low and include the use of a range of facilities, from hot showers to supermarkets and restaurants. A list of camp sites is available on the DCC (German Camping Club) website: **www.camping-club.de**.

phrasemaker

places to stay

das Ferienappartement	*das fayryenappartment*	self-catering apartment
das Gästezimmer	*das gestetsimmer*	guest room/B&B
das Gasthaus	*das gasthows*	guest house
das Hotel	*das hotel*	hotel
der Campingplatz	*der kempingplats*	campsite
der Gasthof	*der gasthohf*	guest house
die Jugendherberge	*dee yoohgentherbayrge*	youth hostel
die Pension	*dee pangzyohn*	boarding house

finding a place & checking in

you may say ...

I have a reservation for a room.	Ich habe ein Zimmer reserviert.	*ish haabe iyn tsimmer rezerveert*
in the name of ...	auf den Namen ...	*owf dayn naamen*
I'd like to book ...	Ich möchte ... reservieren.	*ish mershte ... rezerveeren*
a room.	ein Zimmer	*iyn tsimmer*
a double room.	ein Doppelzimmer	*iyn doppeltsimmer*
Do you have a room?	Haben Sie ein Zimmer frei?	*haaben zee iyn tsimmer friy*

Somewhere to Stay

Do you have ...	Haben Sie ...	*haaben zee*
a single room?	ein Einzelzimmer?	*iyn iyntseltsimmer*
a twin room?	ein Zimmer mit zwei Einzelbetten?	*iyn tsimmer mit tsviy iyntselbetten*
a room with three beds?	ein Dreibettzimmer?	*iyn driybetttsimmer*
for ...	für ...	*fewr*
one/two nights	eine Nacht/zwei Nächte	*iyne nakt/tsviy neshte*
one/two weeks	eine Woche/zwei Wochen	*iyne voke/tsviy voken*
three people	drei Personen	*driy perzohnen*
two adults and a child	zwei Erwachsene und ein Kind	*tsviy ervaksene oont iyn kint*
May I see the room?	Könnte ich das Zimmer sehen?	*kernnte ish das tsimmer zayen*
How much is it ...	Wie viel kostet es ...	*vee feel kostet es*
per night?	pro Nacht?	*proh nakt*
per week?	pro Woche?	*proh voke*
Is there ...	Gibt es ...	*geept es*
a reduction for children?	eine Ermäßigung für Kinder?	*iyne ermayssigoong fewr kinder*
Do you have anything cheaper?	Haben Sie etwas Billigeres?	*haaben zee etvas billigeres*
Do you have wheel-chair-accessible rooms?	Haben Sie rollstuhlgerechte Zimmer?	*haaben zee rollshtoohlgereshte tsimmer*
I'll take it.	Ich nehme es.	*ish nayme es*

you may hear ...

Für wie viele ...	*fewr vee feele*	For how many ...
Nächte?	*neshte*	nights?
Personen?	*perzohnen*	people?
Raucher oder Nichtraucher?	*rowker ohder nishtrowker*	Smoking or non-smoking?
Herzlich willkommen.	*hertslish villkommen*	Welcome.
Tut mir Leid, alle Zimmer sind besetzt.	*tooht meer liyt alle tsimmer zint bezetst*	I'm sorry, we're full.

Kinder bezahlen die Hälfte.	*kinder betsaalen dee helfte*	Children half price.
Hier ist ...	*heer ist*	Here is ...
das Anmeldeformular.	*das anmeldeformoolaar*	the registration form.
der Zimmerschlüssel.	*der tsimmerschlewssel*	the key.
Ihren Namen/Pass, bitte.	*eeren naamen/pass, bitte*	Your name/ passport, please.
Wie ist Ihr Autokennzeichen?	*vee ist eer owtokenntsiyken*	What is your car registration?

check out 1

You're reserving a room in a hotel.

○ Guten Tag. Ich möchte bitte ein Zimmer reservieren.
goohten taag. ish mershte bitte iyn tsimmer rezerveeren

- Selbstverständlich. Für wie viele Nächte?
zelpstfershtendlish. fewr vee feele neshte

○ Für eine Woche, bitte.
fewr iyne voke bitte

- Gut. Ihren Namen, bitte?
gooht. eeren naamen bitte

○ Peter Ganz.
payter gants

- Möchten Sie ein Einzelzimmer?
mershten zee iyn iyntseltsimmer

○ Nein, ein Doppelzimmer, bitte. Was kostet das?
niyn iyn doppeltsimmer bitte. vas kostet das

- Das macht dreihundertdreiundvierzig Euro.
das makt driyhoondert-driyoontfeertsig oyro

Q How long do you want to stay?
What is the total cost?

asking about your room

you may say …

Does the room have …	Hat das Zimmer …	*hat das **tsi**mmer*
a shower?	eine Dusche?	*iyne **doo**she*
a bath?	ein Bad?	*iyn baat*
a cot?	ein Kinderbett?	*iyn **kin**derbett*
a phone?	ein Telefon?	*iyn **te**lefohn*
an internet connection?	Internetzugang?	***in**ternettsoohgang*
cable TV?	Kabelfernsehen?	***kaa**belfernzayen*
Is there …	Gibt es …	*geept es*
a car park?	einen Parkplatz?	***iy**nen **paark**plats*
a bar?	eine Bar?	***iy**ne baar*
a lift?	einen Fahrstuhl?	***iy**nen **faar**shtoohl*
room service?	Zimmerservice?	***tsi**mmerservis*
Is breakfast included?	Ist das Frühstück inklusive?	*ist das **frew**shtewk inkloo**zee**ve*
What time is breakfast?	Wann gibt es Frühstück?	*vann geept es **frew**shtewk*
Where is the …	Wo ist …	*voh ist*
dining room?	das Speisezimmer?	*das **shpiy**zetsimmer*
gym?	der Fitnessraum?	*der **fit**nessrowm*
conference room?	der Konferenzraum?	*der konfe**rents**rowm*
When do I have to check out?	Wann muss ich das Zimmer verlassen?	*vann mooss ish das **tsi**mmer fer**la**ssen*
How do I get an outside number?	Wie telefoniere ich raus?	*vee telefoh**nee**re ish rows*

you may hear ...

Selbstverständlich/ Natürlich.	*zelpstfer**shtend**lish/ na**tewr**lish*	Of course.
Nein, leider nicht.	*niyn **liy**der nisht*	Unfortunately not.
Ihr Zimmer ist ... im ersten Stock. im zweiten Stock. im Erdgeschoss.	*eer **tsi**mmer ist im **ers**ten shtok im **tsviy**ten shtok im **ayrt**geshoss*	Ihr Zimmer ist ... on the first floor. on the second floor. on the ground floor.
Frühstück ist von sieben Uhr dreißig bis neun Uhr.	***frew**shtewk ist fon **zee**ben oohr **driy**ssig bis noyn oohr*	Breakfast is from 7.30am to 9am.
... ist nicht inklusive. Frühstück Mehrwertsteuer	*... ist nisht inkloo**zee**ve **frew**shtewk **mayr**vayrtshtoyer*	... is not included. Breakfast Tax
Wählen Sie Null.	***vay**len zee nooll*	Dial zero.

check out 2

You want to know what time you have to check out.

○ Wann muss ich das Zimmer verlassen?
*vann mooss ish das **tsi**mmer fer**la**ssen*

- Um zehn Uhr. Frühstück ist von sieben Uhr bis neun Uhr.
*oom tsayn oohr. **frew**shtewk ist fon **zee**ben oohr bis noyn oohr*

Q By what time should you check out?
And when is breakfast served?

problems
you may say ...

... is not working.	... funktioniert nicht.	*... foonktsyoneert nisht*
The telephone	Das Telefon	*das telefohn*
The television	Der Fernseher	*der fernzayer*
The iron	Das Bügeleisen	*das bewgeliyzen*
The light	Das Licht	*das lisht*
How do you work ...	Wie funktioniert ...	*vee foonktsyoneert*
the shower?	die Dusche?	*dee dooshe*
the air conditioning?	die Klimaanlage?	*dee kleema-anlaage*
the heating?	die Heizung?	*dee hiytsoong*
There is ... in the room.	Es gibt ... im Zimmer.	*es geept ... im tsimmer*
no soap	keine Seife	*kiyne ziyfe*
no toilet paper	kein Klopapier	*kiyn klohpapeer*
no remote control	keine Fernbedienung	*kiyne fernbedeenoong*
The toilet doesn't flush.	Die Klospülung geht nicht.	*dee klohshpewloong gayt nisht*
There is no hot water.	Ich habe kein warmes Wasser.	*ish haabe kiyn vaarmes vasser*
Can I have another towel?	Kann ich noch ein Handtuch bekommen?	*kann ish nok iyn hanttoohk bekommen*

you may hear ...

Worum geht es denn?	*vohroom gayt es denn*	What is the problem?
Ich schicke jemanden.	*ish shike yaymanden*	I'll send someone.
Ich hole es Ihnen.	*ish hohle es eenen*	I'll get you it/one.

asking for help

you may say ...

Could I have an alarm call at ...?	Können Sie mich bitte um ... telefonisch wecken?	*kernnen zee mish **bitte** oom ... tele**foh**nish ve**ken***
Have you got a ... safe deposit box? map of the town?	Haben Sie einen Safe? Stadtplan?	*haaben zee **iy**nen sayf **shtat**plaan*
Could you recommend a restaurant?	Können Sie ein Restaurant empfehlen?	*kernnen zee iyn resto**rang** emp**fayl**en*
Can you order me a taxi please?	Können Sie mir bitte ein Taxi bestellen?	*kernnen zee meer **bitte** iyn **tak**see be**shtell**en*

checking out

you may say ...

I'd like to pay the bill.	Ich möchte die Rechnung bezahlen.	*ish **mersh**te dee **resh**noong be**tsaal**en*
by ... traveller's cheque credit card cheque	mit ... Reisescheck Kreditkarte Scheck	*mit **riy**zeshek kre**deet**karte shek*
I'll pay cash.	Ich zahle bar.	*ish **tsaal**e baar*
I think there is a mistake.	Ich glaube, da ist ein Fehler.	*ish glowbe, daa ist iyn **fayl**er*

you may hear ...

Welche Zimmernummer?	*velshe **tsi**mmernoommer*	What room number?
Wie möchten Sie zahlen?	*vee **mersh**ten zee **tsaal**en*	How would you like to pay?
Unterschreiben Sie bitte hier.	*oonter**shriy**ben zee **bitte** heer*	Please sign here.

Somewhere to Stay

at the campsite

you may say …

Have you got a site for …	Haben Sie einen Stellplatz für …	*haaben zee iynen shtellplats fewr*
a tent?	ein Zelt?	*iyn tselt*
a caravan?	einen Wohnwagen?	*iynen vohnvaagen*
We are two adults and three children.	Wir sind zwei Erwachsene und drei Kinder.	*veer zint tsviy ervaksene oont driy kinder*
Where are …	Wo sind …	*voh zint*
the showers?	die Duschen?	*dee dooshen*
the dustbins?	die Mülleimer?	*dee mewlliymer*
the toilets?	die Toiletten?	*dee toaletten*
Is there …	Gibt es …	*geept es*
a laundry?	einen Waschsalon?	*iynen vashzalong*
a shop?	ein Geschäft?	*iyn gesheft*
a playground?	einen Spielplatz?	*iynen shpeelplats*
electricity?	Strom?	*shtrohm*
Can we camp here?	Dürfen wir hier zelten?	*dewrfen veer heer tselten*

you may hear …

Wie lange bleiben Sie?	*vee lange bliyben zee*	How long are you going to stay?
Wie viele Personen sind Sie?	*vee feele perzohnen zint zee*	How many people?
Schönen Aufenthalt!	*shernen owfenthalt*	Have a nice stay!
Das macht zehn Euro pro Tag.	*das makt zayn oyro proh taak*	That's €10 per day.

at the youth hostel

you may say ...

I'd like a bed for two nights.	Ich möchte ein Bett für zwei Nächte.	*ish **mersh**te iyn bett fewr tsviy **nesh**te*
Can I hire ... a sleeping bag? some sheets?	Kann ich ... ausleihen? einen Schlafsack Bettwäsche	*kann ish ... **ows**liyhen **iy**nen **shlaaf**zak **bett**veshe*
What time do you lock up?	Um wie viel Uhr wird abgeschlossen?	*oom vee feel oohr wirt **ap**geshlossen*
Is there an internet connection here?	Gibt es hier Internetanschluss?	*geept es heer **in**ternet**an**shlooss*

you may hear ...

| Haben Sie einen Jugendherbergsaus- weis? | *haaben zee **iy**nen yoohgentherbayrk- sowsviys* | Have you got a membership card? |

---

check out 3

You arrive at the campsite reception.

○ Guten Tag. Haben Sie einen Stellplatz für einen Wohnwagen?
*goohten taak. haaben zee **iy**nen **shtell**plats fewr **iy**nen **vohn**vaagen*

– Ja, sicher. Wie viele Personen sind Sie?
*yaa **zi**sher. vee **fee**le per**zoh**nen zint zee*

○ Wir sind zwei Erwachsene und zwei Kinder.
*veer zint tsviy er**vak**sene oont tsviy **kin**der*

– Wie lange bleiben Sie?
*vee **lan**ge **bliy**ben zee*

○ Drei Wochen, bitte.
*driy **vo**ken **bit**te*

Q Do you have a caravan or a tent?
How many of you are there in total?

Somewhere to Stay

signs
you may see ...

Ausgang	exit
Außer Betrieb	out of order
bitte klingeln	ring the bell
drücken	push
Eingang	entry
Halbpension	half board
Notausgang	emergency exit
Parken verboten	parking prohibited
Rauchen verboten	smoking prohibited
(kein) Trinkwasser	(not) drinking water
Vollpension	full board
ziehen	pull

sound check

In German, the 'Umlaut' means that there are three extra vowels – **ä**, **ö** and **ü**. Although they don't exist in the English language, some English sounds come close to them.

ä can be pronounced as a long sound, like the 'ay' in 'pay':
Fensterläden *fensterlayden*   fährt *fayrt*
or as a short sound like the 'e' in 'let':
Nächte *neshte*   Geschäft *gesheft*

ö is pronounced like the 'er' in 'fern' and **ü** is similar to the 'ew' in 'dew':
können *kernnen*   schön *shern*
Frühstück *frewshtewk*   Bügeleisen *bewgeliyzen*

try it out

in the mix
Unscramble the following words – they're all things you might find in a hotel.

1 zimEinzelmer
2 husDec
3 schlüsZimmersel
4 derKinbett
5 herseFern
6 lageKanamil

match it up
Can you match the questions with the right answers?

1 Für wie viele Nächte?
2 Hat das Zimmer Telefon?
3 Wo gibt es Frühstück?
4 Wie viele Personen sind Sie?
5 Haben Sie Zimmer frei?

a Zwei Erwachsene.
b Im Speisezimmer.
c Alle Zimmer sind besetzt.
d Nein, aber einen Fernseher.
e Eine Woche, bitte.

as if you were there
You're checking your family into a hotel. Follow the prompts to play your part.

Herzlich willkommen. Möchten Sie ein Zimmer?
(Say you would like a double and a single room)
Selbstverständlich. Für wie viele Nächte?
(Say for four nights, please. Then ask if the double room has a phone)
Ja, natürlich. Möchten Sie das Zimmer mit Dusche oder Bad?
(Say that you'd like a shower)

linkup

<table>
<tr><td rowspan="7" style="writing-mode: vertical-lr">key phrases</td></tr>
<tr><td>**Haben Sie** ein Zimmer frei?</td><td>**Do you have** a room free?</td></tr>
<tr><td>**Ich möchte** ein Zimmer reservieren.</td><td>**I'd like** to book a room.</td></tr>
<tr><td>**Könnte ich** das Zimmer sehen?</td><td>**Could I** see the room?</td></tr>
<tr><td>**Gibt es** einen Fahrstuhl?</td><td>**Is there** a lift?</td></tr>
<tr><td>**Wo ist** das Speisezimmer?</td><td>**Where is** the dining room?</td></tr>
<tr><td>Die Dusche **funktioniert nicht**.</td><td>The shower **isn't working**.</td></tr>
<tr><td>**Es gibt kein** Handtuch im Zimmer.</td><td>**There is no** towel in the room.</td></tr>
</table>

saying 'no': negatives

The word 'no' is translated as nein when you use it to say 'no' to direct questions:

Haben Sie ein Zimmer frei? - Nein, leider nicht. Have you got a room? - No, unfortunately not.

When you're using it with a noun, to say 'there is no ...', it's translated as kein:

Das Zimmer hat kein Telefon. The room has no telephone.
Ich habe kein Ticket. I have no ticket.

For 'not' you use nicht:

Das Telefon funktioniert nicht. The telephone does not work.
Es ist nicht weit. It's not far.
Ich kann nicht schwimmen. I can't swim.

word order

When saying you'd like to do something (ich möchte ...) or
asking if you could do something (könnte ich ...?), the second
verb goes to the end of the sentence:

Ich möchte ein Zimmer reservieren. I'd like to reserve a room.
Könnte ich das Zimmer sehen? Could I see the room?

The second verb stays in the infinitive or -en form.

For more on word order see the Language Builder, p135. ┈┈┈▷

Buying **Things**

opening hours

German shops can legally open from 6am to 8pm, Monday to Saturday, although in practice supermarkets usually open from around 7am to 7pm, and most other shops tend to open from 9am to 6 or 8pm.

Although some German shopkeepers will bargain over prices, it's not to be recommended. Some do however, offer a discount for cash. Credit cards are accepted by all department stores and most larger shops.

Banks open Monday to Friday from around 8.30am and close between 3pm to 6pm, with an hour's lunch break between 12 and 2pm. Airports and main railway stations have bank branches which open every day as early as 7am and close as late as 10.30pm.

Be advised that some banks don't cash traveller's cheques, so try a **Wechselstube** (exchange bureau) instead.

department stores & shopping arcades

Germany has an impressive range of department stores, from huge individual establishments like Berlin's KaDeWe to country-wide chains such as Kaufhof and Karstadt. Shopping centres are popular, especially during sub-zero winter months. Hamburg has a vast area of inter-connected covered shopping arcades on one bank of the Binnenalster lake.

antique shops

Antique shops in cities and larger towns tend to be concentrated in specific areas, making shopping around easier. Ask at the local tourist office for details.

In Northern Germany, the antique shops of Hamburg, Bremen, Kiel and other coastal towns a great places to find nautical items at knockdown prices.

flea markets

Whether hunting for bargains or simply browsing, a stroll through one of Germany's many bustling **Flohmärkte** (flea markets) is a great experience. You'll find everything from books, clothing and antiques to rare records, military memorabilia and freshly pickled gherkins. The majority of markets take place at the weekend; some of the best-known include:

Munich Huge Saturday market on the site of the former airport, Riem. **www.flohmarkt-riem.com**.

Berlin A wide range of markets to suit all tastes and wallets. Try **Strasse des 17. Juni** for art and handicrafts, or **Kupfergraben** for kitsch souvenirs.

Frankfurt The main Saturday market takes over the Mainufer beside the river.

Hamburg The Sunday fish market has extended over the years into a colourful jumble of stalls offering much more than just North Sea cod.

food markets

A German market isn't just a place to shop – it's a meeting place, where gossip is exchanged and business deals are done across the bare, scrubbed tables of the beer stalls. If you're looking for somewhere to eat well and cheaply, make for the nearest market: the menu includes a juicy slice of local life.

Every town has its weekly market: Berlin has a permanent market in every one of its constituent urban areas, while Munich has two charming markets: the Viktualienmarkt and Elisabethmarkt.

Regional delicacies to look out for include smoked fish and eel in North Germany, and **Schwarzwälder Schinken** (Black Forest ham) in the Black Forest. In wine regions like the Moselle or the Rhineland-Palatinate, look out for good deals on locally-produced wines.

Christmas markets

German **Weihnachtsmärkte** (Christmas markets) are world-famous and there is hardly a town without one. Some, such as the Striezelmarkt in Dresden, have been taking place each December for more than 500 years. Wander around the stalls of handmade Christmas decorations and toys, or join the locals for a sweet snack and delicious hot mug of **Glühwein** (mulled wine).

arts & crafts

Every German region has its own tradition of locally-produced crafts. You'll find glass blowers at work throughout the Bavarian Forest, where you can buy direct from the glassworks and watch your piece taking shape. A long tradition of jewellery-making is undergoing a revival. German potters can be seen at work in backstreet studios of many Bavarian and Black Forest communities. In Bavarian towns like Berchtesgaden and Oberammergau you'll find bearded woodcarvers as gnarled as the wood they're working on. Wooden toys are the speciality of Franconian and Thuringian craft workers, whose products fill the stalls of Germany's lovely Christmas markets.

porcelain & ceramics

The royal porcelain manufacturers of three great German dynasties are still in business, producing some beautiful (and very expensive) items. In Berlin, you can find at the Königliche Porzellanmanufaktur delicate, hand-painted china which once graced the tables of the German royal family. In Munich, Nymphenburg porcelain bears the name of the summer palace of the Wittelsbachs, where fine china is still produced using traditional methods. Meißen is also producing for an expanding export market.

Alternatively, go hunting for a garden gnome among the workshops on the picturesque **Märchenstraße** ('Fairy Tale Route') that stretches from Hanau to Bremen.

phrasemaker

phrases to use anywhere
you may say ...

Where can I buy ...	Wo kann man hier ... kaufen?	*voh kann man heer ... kowfen*
souvenirs?	Souvenirs	*zooveneers*
English newspapers/ magazines?	englische Zeitungen/ Zeitschriften	*englishe tsiytoongen/ tsiytshriften*
Have you got any ...	Haben Sie ...	*haaben zee*
stamps?	Briefmarken?	*breefmarken*
cheese?	Käse?	*kayze*
jeans?	Jeans?	*dsheens*
How much is it (altogether)?	Was kostet das (zusammen)?	*vas kostet das (tsoozammen)*
Can I pay ...	Kann ich ... bezahlen?	*kann ish ... betsaalen*
with traveller's cheques?	mit Reiseschecks	*mit riyzesheks*
by credit card?	mit Kreditkarte	*mit kredeetkarte*
How much is ...	Was kostet/Wie viel kostet ...	*vas kostet/vee feel kostet*
the wine?	der Wein?	*der viyn*
the chocolate?	die Schokolade?	*dee shokolaade*
the sausage?	die Wurst?	*dee voorst*
How much are ...	Was kosten/Wie viel kosten ...	*vas kosten/vee feel kosten*
the CDs?	die CDs?	*dee tsay-days*
the postcards?	die Postkarten?	*dee postkarten*
Where can I buy ...	Wo bekomme ich ...	*voh bekomme ish*
cigarettes?	Zigaretten?	*tsigaretten*
... please.	... bitte.	*... bitte.*
A magazine	Eine Zeitschrift	*iyne tsiytshrift*
A phone card	Eine Telefonkarte	*iyne telefohnkarte*
A map of the town	Einen Stadtplan	*iynen shtatplaan*
Thanks, that's all.	Danke, das ist alles.	*danke das ist alles*

Buying **Things**

you may hear ...

Was kann ich für Sie tun?	*vas kann ish fewr zee toohn*	Can I help you?
Was hätten Sie gern?	*vas hetten zee gern*	What would you like?
Leider nicht.	*liyder nisht*	Unfortunately not.
Bitte schön.	*bitte shern*	There you are.
Dort drüben.	*dort drewben*	Over there.
Sonst noch etwas?	*zonst nok etvas*	Anything else?
Wie viel möchten Sie?	*vee feel mershten zee*	How much would you like?
Das macht ...	*das makt*	That's ... altogether.

check out 1

You're in a souvenir shop in Stuttgart.

- Was kann ich für Sie tun?
  vas kann ish fewr zee toohn

- Haben Sie Schokolade?
  haaben zee shokolaade

- Leider nicht. Sonst noch etwas?
  liyder nisht. zonst nok vas

- Ja, einen Reiseführer von Stuttgart.
  yaa iynen riyzefewrer fon shtoottgart

- Das macht zehn Euro achtzig, bitte.
  das makt tsayn oyro aktsig bitte

Q They have chocolate: true or false?
How much does a travel guide cost?

types of shops

baker's	die Bäckerei	*dee bekeriy*
bookshop	die Buchhandlung	*dee boohkhandloong*
butcher's	der Metzger/der Fleischer	*der metsger/der fliysher*
chemist's	die Apotheke/die Drogerie	*dee apotayke/drogeree*
clothes boutique	das Bekleidungsgeschäft	*das bekliydoongsgesheft*
department store	das Kaufhaus	*das kowfhows*
electronic goods	das Elektrowarengeschäft	*das elektrovaarengesheft*
flea market	der Flohmarkt	*der flohmarkt*
jeweller's	das Schmuckgeschäft/ der Juwelier	*das shmookgesheft/ der yooveleer*
kiosk/news stand	der Kiosk	*der keeosk*
market(square)	der Markt(platz)	*der markt(plats)*
newsagent's	der Zeitschriftenhändler	*der tsiytshriftenhendler*
off licence	der Wein- und Spirituosenladen	*der viyn oont shpiritoo-ohzenlaaden*
optician's	der Optiker	*der optiker*
photographic shop	das Fotogeschäft	*das fohtogesheft*
post office	die Post	*dee post*
shopping centre	das Einkaufszentrum	*das iynkowfstsentroom*
stationer's	der Schreibwarenladen	*der shriypvaarenlaaden*
supermarket	der Supermarkt	*der zoohpermarkt*

Buying **Things**

quantities

you may say …

How much is … it a kilo?	Wie viel kostet … das ein Kilo?	*vee feel **kost**et das iyn **kee**lo*
A kilo of apples, please.	Ein Kilo Äpfel, bitte.	*iyn **kee**lo epfel **bit**te*
half a kilo of grapes	ein Pfund Trauben	*iyn pfoont **trow**ben*
three kilos of oranges	drei Kilo Orangen	*driy **kee**lo orangshen*
100 grammes of ham	einhundert Gramm Schinken	***iyn**hoondert gramm **shin**ken*
a jar of …	ein Glas …	*iyn glaas*
a packet of …	eine Packung …	*iyne pa**koong***
a bottle of …	eine Flasche …	*iyne **fla**she*
a slice of salami	eine Scheibe Salami	*iyne **shiy**be za**laa**mi*
another	noch ein(e)	*nok **iyn**(e)*
a litre/half a litre	ein Liter/ein halber Liter	*iyn **lee**ter/iyn **hal**ber **lee**ter*
Can I try some/a piece?	Kann ich etwas/ein Stück probieren?	*kann ish **et**vas/iyn shtewk pro**bee**ren*
A bit more/less, please.	Ein bisschen mehr/weniger, bitte.	*iyn **biss**shen mayr/**vay**niger **bit**te*
I'll take three, please.	Ich nehme drei Stück, bitte.	*ish **nay**me driy shtewk **bit**te*
I'd like a cheese roll, please.	Ich möchte ein Käsebrötchen, bitte.	*ish **mersh**te iyn **kay**zebrertshen **bit**te*

fruit & vegetables

apples	die Äpfel	dee *epfel*
aubergine	die Aubergine	dee ohber*shee*ne
bananas	die Bananen	dee ba*naa*nen
cabbage	der Weißkohl	der *viyss*kohl
carrots	die Karotten	dee ka*rott*en
cauliflower	der Blumenkohl	der *bloohmen*kohl
cherries	die Kirschen	dee *kir*shen
cucumbers	die Gurken	dee *goor*ken
garlic	der Knoblauch	der *knohp*lowk
grapes	die Trauben	dee *trow*ben
kiwi fruit	die Kiwi	dee *kee*wi
lemons	die Zitronen	dee tsi*trohn*en
lettuce	der Salat	der za*laat*
melon	die Melone	dee me*lohn*e
mushrooms	die Pilze	dee *pilt*se
onions	die Zwiebeln	dee *tsvee*beln
oranges	die Orangen	dee o*rang*shen
peas	die Erbsen	dee *ayrp*sen
peaches	die Pfirsiche	dee *pfirz*ish
pears	die Birnen	dee *birn*en
pepper	die Paprika	dee *paprik*a
plums	die Pflaumen	dee *pflow*men
potatoes	die Kartoffeln	dee kar*toff*eln
red cabbage	der Rotkohl	der *roht*kohl
strawberries	die Erdbeeren	dee *ayrt*bayren
tomatoes	die Tomaten	dee to*maa*ten

Buying **Things**

groceries

bread	das Brot	*das broht*
butter	die Butter	*dee **boo**tter*
cheese	der Käse	*der **kay**ze*
milk	die Milch	*dee milsh*
sausage pâté	die Teewurst	*dee **tay**voorst*
liver pâté	die Leberwurst	*dee **lay**bervoorst*
orange juice	der Orangensaft	*der o**rang**shenzaft*
yoghurt	der Joghurt	*der **yoh**goort*

(For bread, cake and pastries, see the Menu Reader, pp93-97.
For toiletries, see p121.)

buying clothes

you may say …

I'd like …	Ich möchte …	*ish **mersh**te*
a shirt.	ein Hemd.	*iyn hemt*
a pair of trousers.	eine Hose.	*iyne **hoh**ze*
a skirt.	einen Rock.	*iynen rok*
I'm just looking, thank you.	Ich schaue nur, danke.	*ish **show**e noohr **dan**ke*
I'm size …	Ich habe Größe …	*ish **haa**be **grer**sse*
38.	actunddrießig.	*aktoont**driy**ssig*
40.	vierzig.	*feertsig*
42.	zweiundvierzig.	*tsviyoont**feer**tsig*
Have you got size …?	Haben Sie Größe …?	*haaben zee **grer**sse*
Can I try it/them on?	Kann ich es/sie anprobieren?	*kann ish es/zee **an**probeeren*
Where are the changing rooms?	Wo sind die Umkleidekabinen?	*voh zint dee **oom**kliydekabeenen*
It's a bit …	Es ist ein bisschen …	*es ist iyn **biss**shen*
big.	groß.	*grohss*
small.	klein.	*kliyn*
Have you got this …	Haben Sie es …	*haaben zee es*
bigger?	größer?	*grer**sser***
smaller?	kleiner?	*kliy**ner***
cheaper?	billiger?	*billiger*

Do you have the same in ...	Haben Sie das auch in ...	*haaben zee das owk in*
yellow?	Gelb?	*gelp*
cotton?	Baumwolle?	***bowm**volle*
wool?	Wolle?	***vo**lle*
leather?	Leder?	***lay**der*
I (don't) like it.	Es gefällt mir (nicht).	*es ge**fellt** meer (nisht)*
I (don't) like them.	Sie gefallen mir (nicht).	*zee ge**fallen** meer (nisht)*
I'll take ...	Ich nehme ...	*ish **nay**me*
it.	es.	*es*
them.	sie.	*zee*
I'll think about it.	Ich überlege es mir.	*ish ewber**lay**ge es meer*

you may hear ...

Welche Größe/Farbe?	*velshe **grer**sse/**faar**be*	What size/colour?
Gefällt es Ihnen?/ Gefallen sie Ihnen?	*ge**fellt** es **ee**nen/ ge**fallen** zee **ee**nen*	Did you like it/them?
Das kann ich empfehlen.	*das kann ish em**pfay**len*	I can recommend that.

clothes & accessories

belt	der Gürtel	*der **gewr**tel*
boots	die Stiefel	*dee **shtee**fel*
coat	der Mantel	*der **man**tel*
dress	das Kleid	*das kliyt*
gloves	die Handschuhe	*dee **hant**shoohe*
hat	der Hut	*der hooht*
jumper	der Pullover	*der poo**lloh**ver*
jeans	die Jeans	*dee dsheens*

Buying **Things**

scarf	der Schal	*der shaal*
shoes	die Schuhe	*dee shoohe*
socks	die Socken	*dee zoken*
suit (skirt + jacket)	das Kostüm	*das kostewm*
(trouser) suit	der Anzug	*der antsook*
suit jacket	das Jackett	*das dshakett*
swimming costume	der Badeanzug	*der baade-antsook*
tie	die Krawatte	*dee kravatte*
tights	die Strumpfhose	*dee shtroompfhohze*
trunks	die Badehose	*dee baadehohze*
T-shirt	das T-Shirt	*das tee-shirt*

check out 2

You are shopping for some trousers.

○ Ich möchte eine Hose.
ish mershte iyne hohze

- Welche Größe?
velshe grersse

○ Größe vierzig. Haben Sie die auch in blau?
grersse feertsig. haaben zee dee owk in blow

- Ja, hier. Bitte schön.
yaa heer bitte shern.

○ Gut. Ich nehme die Hose, die Handschuhe und das T-Shirt.
gooht. ish nayme dee hohze oont das tee-shirt

- Also, die Hose kostet neunundfünfzig Euro, die Handschuhe zwanzig Euro und das T-Shirt zweiundvierzig Euro.
alzo dee hohze kostet noynoontfewnftsig oyro dee hantshoohe tsrantsig oyro oont das tee-shirt tsviyoontfeertsig oyro

Q What does the assistant ask you?
Which were the most and least expensive items?

at the department store

you may say …

Where is the …	Wo ist die …	*voh ist dee*
department?	abteilung?	*ap**tiy**loong*
ladies'	Damen-	***daa**men*
men's	Herren-	***her**ren*
kids'	Kinder-	***kin**der*
toy	Spielzeug-	***shpeel**tsoyk*
Where do I find …	Wo finde ich …	*voh **fin**de ish*
jumpers?	Pullover?	*poo**lloh**ver*
perfume?	Parfüm?	*par**fewm***
leather goods?	Lederwaren?	***lay**dervaaren*
stationery?	Schreibwaren?	***shriyp**vaaren*
Is there a lift?	Gibt es einen Fahrstuhl?	*geept es **iy**nen **faar**shtoohl*
Where is the checkout?	Wo ist die Kasse?	*voh ist dee **ka**sse*

you may hear …

im Erdgeschoss	*im **ayrt**geshoss*	on the ground floor
im ersten/zweiten/ dritten Stock	*im **ersten**/**tsviy**ten/ **dri**tten shtok*	on the 1st/2nd/3rd floor
im Untergeschoss	*im **oon**tergeshoss*	in the basement
dort drüben	*dort **drew**ben*	over there

Buying **Things**

at the post office
you may say …

Excuse me, where do I have to queue?	Entschuldigung, wo muss ich mich anstellen?	*ent**shool**digoong voh mooss ish mish **an**shtellen*
How much is a … to Great Britain? postcard letter	Was kostet … nach Großbritannien? eine Postkarte ein Brief	*vas **kost**et … nak groh**ssbrit**aanyen* *iyne **post**karte* *iyn breef*
Two stamps, please.	Zwei Briefmarken, bitte.	*tsviy **breef**marken **bi**tte*
Two phone cards for ten Euros, please.	Zwei Telefonkarten zu zehn Euro, bitte.	*tsviy tele**fohn**karten tsooh tsayn **oy**ro **bi**tte*
I'd like to send this to Australia.	Ich möchte das nach Australien schicken.	*ish **mersh**te das nak ow**straa**lyen **shi**ken*
Where is the postbox?	Wo ist der Briefkasten?	*voh ist der **breef**kasten*

check out 3
You go to the post office to buy stamps.

○ Guten Tag. Was kostet eine Postkarte nach England?
*goohten taak. vas **kost**et **iy**ne **post**karte nak **eng**lant*

- Fünfundfünfzig Cent.
*fewnfoont**fewnt**sig tsent*

○ Drei Briefmarken zu fünfundsechzig Cent und eine Telefonkarte zu zehn Euro.
*driy **breef**marken tsooh fewnfoont**zesh**tsig tsent oont **iy**ne tele**fohn**karte tsooh tsayn **oy**ro*

Q How much is it to send a postcard to England?
What do you buy apart from stamps?

getting photos developed

I'd like ... please.	Ich hätte gern ...	*ish **hette** gern*
some batteries	Batterien	*batt**eree**yen*
a disposable camera	eine Wegwerfkamera	*iyne **vek**vayrfkamera*
a memory card	eine Speicherkarte	*iyne **shpiy**sherkarte*
a film for ...	einen Film für ...	*iynen film fewr*
prints	Fotos	*fohtos*
slides	Dias	*deeas*
Can you develop this?	Können Sie das entwickeln lassen?	*kernnen zee das entvikeln lassen*
Can you print from this memory card?	Können Sie Abzüge von dieser Speicherkarte machen?	*kernnen zee aptsewge fon deezer shpiysherkarte maken*
When can I pick it/them up?	Wann kann ich es/sie abholen?	*vann kann ish es/zee aphohlen*

Vierundzwanzig oder sechsunddreißig Bilder?	*feeroonttsvantsig ohder zeksoontdriyssig bilder*	24 or 36 exposures?
Wie groß wollen Sie die Bilder?	*vee grohss vollen zee dee bilder*	What size do you want your prints?
Matt oder Hochglanz?	*matt ohder hohkglants*	Matt or glossy?
heute	*hoyte*	today
morgen	*morgen*	tomorrow
in einer Stunde	*in iyner shtoonde*	in an hour
in zwei Stunden	*in tsviy shtoonden*	in two hours

Buying **Things**

sound check

Note that **v** and **w** are not pronounced the same as in English. At the beginning of a word, **v** sounds like an 'f'.

viel *feel*   voll *foll*

In the middle of a word, however, **v** sounds like the 'v' in 'voice'.

inklusive *inkloo***zee***ve*

w is always pronounced like the 'v' in 'voice':

Wolle *vo**lle***   Leberwurst *lay**bervoorst***

try it out

money talk

Add up what the items below cost.

two chocolate bars – achtzig Cent
an English newspaper – drei Euro fünfundfünfzig
two postcards – ein Euro
Das kostet zusammen: ... Euro

as if you were there

You're at the market stall, buying fruit for a picnic. Follow the prompts to play your part.

Guten Tag. Was kann ich für Sie tun?
(Ask how much the cherries are)
Ein Kilo, vier Euro zwanzig.
(Say two kilos, please)
Bitte schön.
(Ask if she has any strawberries)
Ja. Wie viel möchten Sie?
(Say 300 grammes)
Sonst noch etwas?
(Say that's all, thanks)

linkup

Haben Sie Briefmarken?	**Have you got** any stamps?
Wo bekomme ich Telefonkarten?	**Where do I get** telephone cards?
Was kostet der Reiseführer?	**How much is** the travel guide?
Ich möchte eine Bluse.	**I'd like** a blouse.
Der Hut **gefällt mir/ gefällt mir nicht**.	**I like** the hat/**I don't like** the hat.
Ich nehme ein Kilo.	**I'll take** a kilo.

asking where to find things

If you would like to know where you can find something, you can simply say:

Ich suche eine Buchhandlung. I am looking for a bookshop.

You can also use this phrase when looking for objects:

Ich suche meine Jacke. I am looking for my jacket.

Alternatively, you can ask questions like:

Wo ist hier eine Buchhandlung? Where is there a bookshop (around) here?

Wo finde ich eine Buchhandlung? Where can I find a bookshop?

It's polite to add Entschuldigung (Excuse me) at the beginning of the sentence.

If you're in a shop and want to know where to find something in particular, you can simply ask:

Wo sind die Schuhe? Where are the shoes?

Wo finde ich Schuhe? Where do I find shoes?

Wo bekomme ich Schuhe? Where do I get shoes?

Buying Things

If you want to know if a shop sells a certain item, you can say:
Haben Sie Briefmarken? Do you sell stamps?
Another common way of saying the same thing is:
Führen Sie Briefmarken? (literally, Do you stock stamps?)
Note that the word 'any' is usually not translated when you ask if a shop sells something:
Haben Sie CDs? Do you have any CDs?

prices

There are two ways of asking how much something costs:
Was kostet das T-Shirt? How much is the T-Shirt? (literally, What does the T-shirt cost?)
Wie viel kosten die Tomaten? How much are the tomatoes?
Use kostet when referring to one thing, and kosten for more than one.

saying what you like

There are different ways of saying what you like or dislike. You can say:
Das Kleid **gefällt mir**. I like this dress.
or the opposite:
Das Kleid **gefällt mir nicht**. I don't like this dress.
Note how the sentence structure is different to the English (literally, The dress is pleasing to me).
The ending of the verb changes if you are talking about more than one thing:
Die Schuhe **gefallen** mir. I like these shoes.

You can also use the word mag to say that you like something:
Ich mag Schokolade. I like chocolate.

If you want to say that you enjoy doing something you use the word 'gern':
Ich lese gern. I like reading.

Café **Life**

cafés

Germans love their **Kaffee und Kuchen** (coffee and cakes), and you'll find plenty of relaxed cafés where you can sit and while away an afternoon sampling a wide selection of pastries. Cafés range from elegant Viennese coffee houses to small establishments attached to bakeries and chain branches in department stores. Most serve light savoury snacks as well as cakes and ice cream, and often have outdoor seating during the summer months. Cafés tend to stay open all day, though the traditional time to stop for coffee and a snack is mid-afternoon. Look for a **Konditorei** (café), **Eisdiele** (ice cream parlour) or **Imbiss** (snack bar).

bars

Germany has plenty of great places to drink, ranging from huge **Bierkeller** (beer halls) in Bavaria to **Biergärten** (beer gardens) and bars of all kinds and sizes. Beer gardens are usually open from lunchtime to about midnight and offer a variety of beers and some hearty dishes. Opening times for pubs and bars vary, but most stay open till 2 or 3am, and some have 24 hour licensing. There are about 5000 German beers for you to sample, including Bavaria's **Weißbier** (white beer), **Schwarzbier**, the malted black beer brewed in Thuringia and Saxony, and the strong **Bockbier**.

phrasemaker

ordering

you may say ...

I'd like a piece of ...	Ich möchte ein Stück ...	*ish **mersh**te iyn shtewk*
apple cake.	Apfelkuchen.	*apfelkoohken*
cream cake.	Sahnetorte.	*zaanetorte*
Have you got any ...	Haben Sie ...	*haaben zee*
strawberry ice cream?	Erdbeereis?	*ayrtbayriys*
mineral water?	Mineralwasser?	*mineraalvasser*
What ... do you have?	Was für ... haben Sie?	*vas fewr ... haaben zee*
soft drinks	alkoholfreie Getränke	*alkohohlfriye getrenke*
cakes	Kuchen	*koohken*
ice creams	Eis	*iys*
I'd like a cup of ...	Ich möchte eine Tasse ...	*ish mershte iyne tasse*
tea.	Tee.	*tay*
I'll have a pot of coffee.	Ich nehme ein Kännchen Kaffee.	*ish nayme iyn kennshen kaffay*
with ...	mit ...	*mit*
sugar	Zucker	*tsooker*
milk	Milch	*milsh*
lemon	Zitrone	*tsitrohne*
ice	Eis	*iys*
This one, please.	Diesen hier, bitte.	*deezen heer, bitte*
Do you serve outside?	Bedienen Sie draußen?	*bedeenen zee drowssen*

you may hear ...

| Was möchten Sie, bitte? | *vas **mersh**ten zee **bi**tte* | What would you like? |
| Was trinken Sie? | *vas **trin**ken zee* | What would you like to drink? |

73

Tut mir Leid, wir haben kein ... mehr.	*tooht meer liyt veer haaben kiyn ... mayr*	Sorry, we've run out of ...
Kommt sofort!	*kommt zofort*	Right away!
Kännchen oder Tasse?	*kennshen ohder tasse*	A small pot or a cup?
Mit Milch oder schwarz?	*mit milsh ohder shvarts*	With milk or black?
mit ...	*mit*	with ...
Sahne	*zaane*	cream
Schlagsahne	*shlaakzaane*	whipped cream
Mit Kohlensäure oder ohne Kohlensäure?	*mit kohlenzoyre ohder ohne kohlenzoyre*	Sparkling or still?
Welchen?	*velshen*	Which one?
Wie viele Kugeln?	*vee feele koohgeln*	How many scoops?
Wir haben ... eis.	*veer haaben ... iys*	We've got ... ice cream.
Kirsch-	*kirsh*	cherry
Vanille-	*vanille*	vanilla
Pistazien-	*pistaatseeyen*	pistachio
Welche Sorte?	*velshee zorte*	What flavour?
Bitte zahlen Sie an der Kasse.	*bitte tsaalen zee an der kasse*	Please pay at the till.

check out 1

You've stopped for a snack while out shopping.

○ Haben Sie Obstkuchen?
haaben zee ohpstkoohken

- Ja, Apfelkuchen. Und was trinken Sie?
yaa apfelkoohken. oont vas trinken zee

○ Eine Tasse heiße Schokolade, bitte.
iyne tasse hiysse shokolaade bitte

- Kommt sofort!
kommt zofort

Q What type of fruit cake are you offered?
What do you order to drink?

bread, cake & pastries

der Apfelstrudel	der *apfelshtroohdel*	apple strudel
das Bauernbrot	das *bowernbroht*	bread made from sourdough
der Berliner	der *berleener*	doughnut
der Bienenstich	der *beenenshtish*	sticky pastry filled with sweet cream
die Brezel	dee *braytsel*	pretzel
das Brot	das *broht*	bread
das Brötchen	das *brertshen*	bread roll
das Hörnchen	das *hernshen*	type of croissant
die Marzipantorte	dee *martsipaantorte*	marzipan gâteau
der Mohnkuchen	der *mohnkoohken*	poppy seed cake
die Nusstorte	dee *noosstorte*	cream gâteau with nuts
der Obstkuchen	der *ohpstkoohken*	fruit cake
der Pumpernickel	der *poompernikel*	heavy, dark bread
die Sachertorte	dee *zakertorte*	chocolate gâteau
die Schokoladentorte	dee *shokolaadentorte*	chocolate cake
das Schwarzbrot	das *shvartsbroht*	dark bread
die Schwarzwälder Kirschtorte	dee *shvartsvelder kirshtorte*	Black Forest gâteau
der Streuselkuchen	der *shtroyzelkoohken*	crumble cake
das Vollkornbrot	das *follkornbroht*	heavy, wholemeal bread
der Zwetschgenkuchen	der *tsvetshgenkoohken*	type of plum cake

hot drinks

black coffee	der schwarze Kaffee	*der shvartse kaffay*
coffee with milk	der Kaffee mit Milch	*der kaffay mit milsh*
strong black coffee	der Mokka	*der mokka*
latte	der Milchkaffee	*milshkaffee*
cappuccino	der Cappuccino	*der kappootsheeno*
decaffeinated	entkoffeiniert	*entkoffay-eeneert*
espresso	der Espresso	*der espresso*
... tea	der ... tee	*der ... tay*
fruit	Früchte-	*frewshte-*
mint	Pfefferminz-	*pfeffermints-*
camomile	Kamillen-	*kamillentay*
hot chocolate	die heiße Schokolade	*dee hiysse shokolaade*
weak/strong	schwache/starke	*shvake/shtarke*

soft drinks

alcohol-free beer	das alkoholfreie Bier	*das alkohohlfriye beer*
freshly-squeezed apple/grapefruit juice	der frisch gepresste Apfelsaft/ Grapefruitsaft	*der frish gepresste apfelzaft/ graypfroohtzaft*
(diet) Coke	die Cola (light)	*dee kohla (liyt)*
fizzy orange	die Orangenlimonade	*dee orangshenlimonaade*
iced coffee	der Eiskaffee	*der iyskaffay*
lemonade	die Limonade	*dee limonaade*
milkshake	der Milchshake	*der milshshayk*
tonic water	das Tonicwasser	*das tonikvasser*
sparkling/still mineral water	das Mineralwasser mit Kohlensäure/ ohne Kohlensäure	*das mineraalvasser mit kohlenzoyre/ohne kohlenzoyre*

measures

bottle	die Flasche	*dee flashe*
can	die Dose	*dee dohze*
glass	das Glas	*das glaas*
jug	die Karaffe	*dee karaffe*
mug	der Becher	*der besher*

Café **Life**

alcoholic drinks

... wine	der ... wein	*der ... viyn*
white/red/rosé	Weiß-/Rot-/Rosé-	*viyss/roht/rozay*
house/table wine	Haus-/Tafel	*hows/taafel*
dry/sweet	trockene/liebliche	*trokene/leeplishe*
sparkling wine	der Sekt	*der zekt*
spritzer	die Weinschorle	*dee viynshorle*
medium dry wine	der Auslesewein	*der owslayzeviyn*
... beer	das ... Bier	*das ... beer*
blond/dark	helle/dunkle	*helle/doonkle*
draught/bottled	Fass-/Flaschen-	*fass/flashen*
bitter	Alt-	*alt-*
sweet malt beer	das Malzbier	*das maltsbeer*
light ale (with raspberry syrup)	die Berliner Weiße (mit Schuss)	*dee berleener viysse (mit shooss)*
light wheat beer	das Weizenbier	*das viytsenbeer*
brandy	der Weinbrand	*der viynbrant*
champagne	der Champagner	*der shampanyer*
cider	der Apfelwein	*der apfelviyn*
gin and tonic	der Gin und Tonic	*der dshin oont tonik*
kirsch	das Kirschwasser	*das kirshvasser*
lager	das Pils	*das pils*
liqueurs	Liköre	*leekerre*
port	der Portwein	*der portviyn*
shandy	das Radler	*das raatler*
sherry	der Sherry	*der sherree*
whisky	der Whisky	*der viskee*

check out 2

You're ordering cake, but your first choice is not available.

○ Ein Stück Schwarzwälder Kirschtorte.
*iyn shtewk **shvart**svelder **kirsht**orte*

- Tut mir Leid. Das haben wir nicht. Möchten Sie Schokoladentorte?
*tooht meer liyt. das **haab**en veer nisht. **mersh**ten zee shoko**laad**entorte*

○ Nein, danke.
*niyn **dank**e*

Q   You order chocolate cake: true or false?

sound check

ch has three different possible pronunciations in German. After **a**, **o**, **u** and **au**, **ch** is a hard sound, somewhere between the 'k' in 'kit' and the 'ch' in 'loch':

Kuchen   *koohken*   rauchen   *rowken*

If **ch** is followed by **s** it is pronounced like the 'x' in 'taxi':

sechs   *zeks*   nächste   *naykste*

Otherwise, it sounds like a softer version of 'sh' in 'shut':

Kännchen   *kennshen*   möchten   *mershten*

Café **Life**

question time

Find the matching response to each sentence. They're all things you might say in a café.

1 Ich möchte Mineralwasser.
- **a** Welchen Geschmack?
- **b** Mit Kohlensäure?
- **c** Kännchen oder Tasse?

2 Ich nehme Kaffee, bitte.
- **a** Das macht 1,80 Euro, bitte.
- **b** Mit oder ohne Kohlensäure?
- **c** Und was trinken Sie?

3 Welche alkoholfreien Getränke haben Sie?
- **a** Wir haben Bier und Limonade.
- **b** Mineralwasser, Limonade, Cola …
- **c** Erdbeereis, Schokoladentorte.

4 Haben Sie Obstkuchen?
- **a** Ja, die Schokoladentorte ist gut.
- **b** Mit Zitrone?
- **c** Ja, Apfelkuchen.

in the mix

This conversation in a café is jumbled up. Can you put the phrases in the right order?

- **a** Eine Tasse, bitte.
- **b** Selbstverständlich. Und was trinken Sie?
- **c** Ein Stück Apfelkuchen, bitte.
- **d** Kommt sofort.
- **e** Kaffee, bitte.
- **f** Guten Tag, was bekommen Sie?
- **g** Kännchen oder Tasse?

as if you were there

You order coffee and cake in a café. Follow the prompts to play your part.

Guten Tag. Was bekommen Sie?
(Say you'd like a piece of apple cake)
Tut mir Leid. Das haben wir nicht.
(Ask if they have chocolate cake)
Ja. Und was trinken Sie?
(Say you'd like a cup of coffee)
Kommt sofort!

linkup

Haben Sie Eis?	**Do you have** any ice cream?
Ein Stück Torte, bitte.	**A piece of** cake, please.
Ich nehme den Apfelkuchen.	**I'll take** the apple cake.
Ich möchte einen Kaffee.	**I'd like** a coffee.
Was für belegte Brote **haben Sie**?	**What** sandwiches **do you have**?

requesting things

The easiest way is simply to say what you want:
Ein Bier (bitte).   A beer (please).

You can add 'please', even though it's less common than in English.

You can also say:

Ich möchte ein Mineralwasser, bitte.
Ich nehme einen Kaffee.
Ich hätte gern eine heiße Schokolade.
Ich bekomme ein Bier. **(literally, I'm getting a beer)**

All these are equivalent to the English 'Please could I have ...?'.

more than one

If you are talking about more than one of something, the word usually changes its ending, for example:
die Torte, die Torten the cake, the cakes

The German word for 'the' is die in the plural.
Sometimes an **-e** is added to the noun:
der Schuh, die Schuhe

Sometimes even the middle of the word can change:
das Glas, die Gläser

And in some cases the ending does not change at all:
der Kuchen, die Kuchen

But when you're ordering food and drink, the word remains the same:
Zwei Bier, bitte. Two beers, please.
Drei Glas Wein. Three glasses of wine.

For more on plurals see the Language Builder, p133. ┄┄┄>

Eating **Out**

Germans love to eat out, and some city restaurants are so busy that they never close. Restaurants, pubs and bars all welcome children, and many provide children's menus. In most resorts and spas, specially-priced **Seniorenteller** (dishes for senior citizens) can be requested by elderly visitors.

meals

Breakfast Germans traditionally eat a very hearty breakfast, and this is catered for by cafés and early-opening bars. In Hamburg, late-night revellers can eat freshly-caught fish at quayside bars, while in Bavaria some workers have a morning break to tuck into **Weißwurst** (local white sausage, not supposed to be eaten after midday) and pretzels.

Lunch After such a heavy breakfast, lunch breaks and menus are consequently short.

Dinner Evening meals are served relatively early, from about 7pm on, but kitchens generally stay open until midnight or later.

where to eat

It is well-worth choosing a hotel or pension which offers a buffet-style breakfast. You can then eat a typically German light lunch. In the city this means eating at a market stall or at any of the German, Greek or Turkish delicatessens which line central streets. In the country, go to a local inn (if there's a **Gasthof zur Post** make for that as the food and beer are almost always excellent).

A typical restaurant or tavern menu will have soup as a starter (German soups are deservedly famous) and a meat-based dish (usually pork or veal) as a main course.

vegetarians

Germany is historically a nation of meat-eaters, but there are now vegetarian restaurants in all large towns, and a choice of vegetarian dishes in most restaurants.

phrasemaker

finding somewhere to eat
you may say ...

Is there a good restaurant nearby?	Gibt es ein gutes Restaurant in der Nähe?	*geept es iyn goohtes restorang in der naye*
I'd like to book a table for ...	Ich möchte einen Tisch für ... reservieren.	*ish mershte iynen tish fewr ... rezerveeren*
tomorrow night.	morgen Abend	*morgen aabent*
this evening at 8.30pm.	heute Abend acht Uhr dreißig	*hoyte aabent akt oohr driyssig*
four people.	vier Personen	*feer perzohnen*

arriving
you may say ...

A table for ...	Einen Tisch für ...	*iynen tish fewr*
one person.	eine Person.	*iyne perzohn*
two people.	zwei Personen.	*tsviy perzohnen*
We have a reservation.	Wir haben eine Reservierung.	*veer haaben iyne rezerveeroong*
Is this table free?	Ist dieser Tisch noch frei?	*ist deezer tish nok friy*
Do you have a high chair?	Haben Sie einen Babystuhl?	*haaben zee iynen baybeeshtoohl*
Excuse me, is this self-service?	Entschuldigung, ist hier Selbstbedienung?	*entshooldigoong ist heer zelpstbedeenoong*

Hausgemachter
Wurstsalat 5,80
mit Brot
Bratwurst 5,50
mit Bratkartoffeln
2 Weisswürste
mit Brezeln 4,80

you may hear ...

Einen Moment, bitte.	*iynen moment bitte*	One moment, please.
Sie müssen warten.	*zee mewssen varten*	You'll have to wait.
Wir sind heute Abend ausgebucht.	*veer zint hoyte aabent owsgeboohkt*	Sorry, we're full for tonight.
Raucher oder Nichtraucher?	*rowker ohder nishtrowker*	Smoking or non-smoking?

check out 1

You ask for a table at a restaurant.

○ Guten Tag, einen Tisch für drei Personen, bitte.
  goohten taak iynen tish fewr driy perzohnen bitte

- Einen Moment, bitte. Sie müssen zehn Minuten warten.
  iynen moment bitte. zee mewssen tsayn minoohten varten

Q How many people are eating?
   How long do you have to wait?

Eating **Out**

asking about the menu
you may say ...

The menu, please.	Die Speisekarte, bitte.	*dee **shpiy**zekarte **bi**tte*
What is the special today?	Was ist das Tagesgericht?	*vas ist das **taa**gesgerisht*
What is ... ?	Was ist ... ?	*vas ist*
Can you recommend anything?	Können Sie etwas empfehlen?	***ker**nen zee **et**vas emp**fay**len*
Do you have ...	Haben Sie ...	***haa**ben zee*
vegetarian dishes?	vegetarische Gerichte?	*vege**taa**rishe ge**rish**te*
a kids' menu?	eine Kinderkarte?	*iyne **kin**derkarte*
I'm allergic to ...	Ich bin gegen ... allergisch.	*ish bin gaygen a**llayr**gish*
nuts.	Nüsse	***new**sse*
cow's milk.	Kuhmilch	***koo**milsh*
I'm ...	Ich bin ...	*ish bin*
vegetarian.	Vegetarier(in).	*vege**taa**ryer(in)*
diabetic.	Diabetiker(in).	*deea**bay**tiker(in)*
Does it contain ...?	Ist das mit ...?	*ist das mit*

ordering
you may say ...

I'd like to order.	Ich möchte bestellen.	*ish **mersh**te be**shte**llen*
I'd like ...	Ich möchte ...	*ish **mersh**te*
a grilled sausage with chips.	eine Bratwurst mit Pommes frites.	*iyne **braat**voorst mit pomm frits*
a pork chop with potatoes.	ein Kotelett mit Kartoffeln.	*iyn kot**lett** mit kar**to**ffeln*
a slice of pizza.	ein Stück Pizza.	*iyn shtewk **pit**sa*
a small/large salad.	einen kleinen/ großen Salat.	*iynen **kliy**nen/ **groh**ssen za**laat***
with ketchup/ mustard	mit Ketchup/Senf	*mit **ket**shap/zenf*

... please.	... bitte.	... *bitte*
A curry sausage,	Eine Currywurst	*iyne **ker**ryvoorst*
A large frankfurter,	Eine Bockwurst	*iyne **bok**voorst*
A kebab,	Ein Schaschlik	*iyn **shash**lik*
A ham sausage,	Eine Schinkenwurst	*iyne **shin**kenvoorst*
I'll take the ...	Ich nehme ...	*ish **nay**me*
chicken with rice.	das Hähnchen mit Reis.	*das **hayn**shen mit riys*
roast beef with potatoes and vegetables.	den Rinderbraten mit Kartoffeln und Gemüse.	*dayn **rinder**braaten mit kar**tof**feln oont ge**mewz**e*
I would like it ...	Ich hätte es gern ... durchgebraten.	*ish **he**tte es gern **doorsh**gebraaten*
rare.	nicht	*nisht*
medium.	halb	*halp*
well done.	gut	*gooht*
I'll have (...) as a ...	Ich nehme (...) als ...	*ish **nay**me (...) als*
starter.	Vorspeise.	***fohr**shpiyze*
main course.	Hauptspeise.	***howpt**shpiyze*
side dish.	Beilage.	***biy**laage*
No dessert, thank you.	Keinen Nachtisch, danke.	***kiy**nen **naak**tish **dan**ke*

you may hear ...

Haben Sie schon gewählt?	*haaben zee shohn ge**wayl**t*	Have you chosen?
Was bekommen Sie?	*vas be**kom**men zee*	What would you like?
Heute haben wir ...	***hoy**te **haa**ben veer*	Today we have ...
Wie möchten Sie das?	*vee **mersh**ten zee das*	How would you like it?
Tut mir Leid, wir haben kein ...	*tooht meer liyt veer **haa**ben kiyn*	Sorry, we don't have any ...
Es ist ...	*es ist*	It's ...
Fleisch.	*fliysh*	meat.
Fisch.	*fish*	fish.
ein Gemüse.	*iyn ge**mewz**e*	a vegetable.
eine Soße.	*iyne **zoh**sse*	a sauce.
Guten Appetit!	***gooh**ten appe**teet***	Enjoy your meal!

check out 2

You ask for a menu, then order your meal.

- Die Speisekarte, bitte.
  *dee **shpiy**zekarte **bi**tte*

○ Schön!
  shern

  (a few minutes later)

○ Haben Sie schon gewählt?
  *haaben zee shohn ge**vaylt***

- Ja, ich möchte bestellen.
  *yaa ish **mersh**te be**shte**llen*

○ Wir haben ein Tagesgericht. Möchten Sie das?
  *veer **haa**ben iyn **taa**gesgerisht. **mersh**ten zee das*

- Können Sie das empfehlen?
  ***ker**nnen zee das em**pfay**len*

○ Das ist sehr gut. Hähnchen mit Reis.
  *das ist zayr gooht. **hayn**shen mit riys*

- Gut, das nehme ich.
  *gooht das **nay**me ish*

Q What does the waitress recommend?
Is today's special pork, chicken or beef?

87

ordering drinks

you may say …

The wine list, please.	Die Weinkarte, bitte.	*dee **viyn**karte **bi**tte*
I'll have …	Ich trinke …	*ish **trin**ke*
a small beer.	ein kleines Bier.	*iyn **kliy**nes beer*
large beer.	ein großes Bier.	*iyn **groh**sses beer*
a mineral water.	ein Mineralwasser.	*iyn mine**raal**vasse*
a bottle	eine Flasche	*iyne **fla**she*
half a bottle	eine halbe Flasche	*iyne **hal**be **fla**she*
a glass of …	ein Glas …	*iyn glaas*
red wine	Rotwein	***roht**viyn*
white wine	Weißwein	***viyss**viyn*
rosé	Roséwein	*ro**zay**viyn*
orange juice	Orangensaft	*orang**shen**zaft*
lemonade	Limonade	*limo**naa**de*

(For more drinks see Café Life, pp76-77.)

you may hear …

| Was trinken Sie? | *vas **trin**ken zee* | What are you drinking? |

check out 3

You would like to order some drinks with your food.

○ Was trinken Sie?
  *vas **trin**ken zee*

- Weißwein, bitte.
  ***viyss**viyn **bi**tte*

○ Ein Glas oder eine Flasche?
  *iyn glaas **oh**der iyne **fla**she*

- Eine Flasche, bitte.
  *iyne **fla**she **bi**tte*

Q What choice do you have to make?

Eating **Out**

during the meal

you may say ...

Excuse me!	Entschuldigung!	*ent**shool**digoong*
I didn't order ...	Ich habe kein ... bestellt.	*ish **haa**be kiyn ... be**shtellt***
Another bottle of/ glass of ...	Noch eine Flasche/ ein Glas ...	*nok **iy**ne flashe/iyn glass*
More ... please. bread wine water	Noch etwas ... bitte. Brot Wein Wasser	*nok **et**vas ... **bit**te broht viyn **va**sser*
The food is ... cold. underdone.	Das Essen ist ... kalt. roh.	*das **e**ssen ist kalt roh*
Thank you, the food was very nice.	Danke, das Essen war sehr gut.	*danke das **e**ssen waar zayr gooht*

you may hear ...

Für wen ist ... das Steak? die Suppe?	*fewr vayn ist das shtayk dee **zoo**ppe*	Who is the ... for? steak soup
Ist alles in Ordnung?	*ist alles in **ort**noong*	Is everything okay?
Hat es Ihnen gesmekt?	*hat es **ee**nen ge**shmekt***	Did you enjoy it?
Darf es noch etwas sein?	*daarf es nok **et**vas ziyn*	Would you like anything else?

on your table

ashtray	der Aschenbecher	*der **a**shenbesher*
bowl (dessert)	die Schale	*dee **shaa**le*
bowl (soup)	der Suppenteller	*der **zoo**ppenteller*
knife/fork	das Messer/die Gabel	*das **me**sser/dee **gaa**bel*
napkin	die Serviette	*dee zer**vye**tte*
plate	der Teller	*der **te**ller*
salt/pepper	das Salz/der Pfeffer	*das zalts/der **pfe**ffer*
spoon/teaspoon	der Löffel/Teelöffel	*der **ler**ffel/**tay**lerffel*
tablecloth	die Tischdecke	*dee **tish**deke*

paying the bill

you may say ...

I'd like to pay.	Ich möchte zahlen.	*ish mershte tsaalen*
The bill, please.	Die Rechnung, bitte.	*dee reshnoong bitte*
Is service included?	Ist das mit Bedienung?	*ist das mit bedeenoong*
Do you take credit cards?	Nehmen Sie Kreditkarten?	*naymen zee kredeetkarten*
There is a mistake, I think.	Ich glaube, da ist ein Fehler.	*ish glowbe daa ist iyn fayler*
We didn't have ...	Wir hatten ...	*veer hatten*
any beer.	kein Bier.	*kiyn beer*
any dessert.	keinen Nachtisch.	*kiynen naaktish*
Keep the change.	Stimmt so.	*shtimmt zoh*

you may hear ...

| Die Bedienung ist nicht inbegriffen/extra. | *dee bedeenoong ist nisht inbegriffen/ekstra* | Service is not included/extra. |

check out 4

It's time to pay for your meal.

○ Hat es Ihnen geschmeckt?
hat es eenen geshmekt

- Ja, das Essen war sehr gut.
yaa das essen vaar zayr gooht

○ Darf es noch etwas sein?
daarf es nok etvas ziyn

- Nein, danke. Ich möchte zahlen.
niyn danke. ish mershte tsaalen

Q What two questions does the waitress ask?

Eating **Out**

sound check

The sounds **ei** and **ie** can easily get mixed up as they look so similar. Remember that **ei** sounds like the 'i' in 'pile', while **ie** is a longer sound, like the 'ee' in 'meet'. Compare the following examples:

Vorspeise *fohrshpiyze*   heißen *hiyssen*

reservieren *rezerveeren*   Bedienung *bedeenoong*

try it out

match it up

Match the English words with their German equivalents.

1	red wine	**a**	Gemischter Salat
2	a cup of coffee	**b**	Apfelkuchen
3	potato salad	**c**	Kartoffelsalat
4	fish	**d**	Rotwein
5	apple cake	**e**	Fisch
6	mixed salad	**f**	eine Tasse Kaffee

as if you were there

In a small restaurant, you're about to order your meal. Follow the prompts to play your part.

(Ask for the menu)
Bitte schön.
(Say that you would like to order)
Was bekommen Sie?
(Ask if she can recommend anything)
Ja, der Bratfisch mit Kartoffelsalat ist gut.
(You don't like fish, so say thank you and order a pork chop with potatoes and a salad)
(later)
Hat es Ihnen geschmeckt?
(Say that the food was good and that you would like to pay)

linkup

key phrases		
Ich nehme den Rinderbraten.	**I'll have** the roast beef.
Ich trinke ein Glas Rotwein.	**I'll have** (literally, I'll drink) a glass of red wine.
Haben Sie Kartoffelsalat?	**Do you have** any potato salad?
Was ist das Tagesgericht?	**What is** the special of the day?
Was sind Dampfnudeln?	**What are** 'Dampfnudeln'?
Noch etwas Wein, bitte.	**Some more** wine, please.

talking to 'you'

In German there is a formal and an informal way of addressing people. The formal/polite words for 'you' are Sie/Ihnen, and the informal words for 'you' are du/dir.

To a waiter in a restaurant you would say:
Haben **Sie** Kartoffelsalat? Do you have any potato salad?
But to a person you know fairly well you might say:
Hast **du** ein Auto? Do you have a car?
Similarly you would say to someone you hardly know:
Wie geht es **Ihnen**? How are you?
But if you want to ask a friend, you would say:
Wie geht es **dir**? How are you?

ordering drinks

Note that in German there is no word for 'of' in phrases like:
Ich trinke ein Glas Wein. I'll have a glass of wine.
Eine Flasche Bier, bitte. A bottle of beer, please.

courses & menus

Vorspeise starter
Hauptspeise/Hauptgericht main dish
Beilage side dish
Nachspeise/Dessert/Nachtisch dessert
Tagesgedeck set menu
Tagesgericht dish of the day
Spezialität des Hauses speciality of the house
Touristenmenü tourist menu

main cooking styles

gekocht boiled
gebraten fried
gegrillt grilled
gedämpft sautéed
gefüllt filled
gedünstet steamed
geräuchert smoked
gewürzt spicy
hausgemacht home-made
Jägerart served in red wine sauce with mushrooms

starters & mains

Aal (in Gelee) (jellied) eel
Austern oysters
Beefsteak mit Zwiebelringen steak with onions
Beefsteak Tartare raw minced steak
Berner Platte sauerkraut with various cooked meats
Birnen, Bohnen und Speck stew with pears, beans, bacon
Blauer Karpfen blue carp
Blaukraut red cabbage
Blumenkohl cauliflower
Blutwurst black pudding
Bockwurst large frankfurter
Bohnen beans
Bouletten hamburgers
Braten roast meat
Bratfisch mit Kartoffelsalat fried fish with potato salad
Brathähnchen roast chicken
Bratkartoffeln fried potatoes
Bratwurst grilled sausage
Bratwurst im Schlafrock sausage roll
Brokkoli broccoli
Brotsuppe bread soup
Buttermilch buttermilk
Currywurst curried sausage
Dampfnudeln steamed dumplings
Dillsoße dill sauce
Dorsch cod
Eintopf stew
Eisbein pig's trotter
Ente duck
Entenbrust duck breast
Erbsen peas
Espresso espresso
Essig vinegar
Fasan mit Weinkraut pheasant with sauerkraut cooked in wine
Fisch fish
Fischfrikadellen fish cakes
Fleischgerichte meat dishes
Fleischpflanzerl meatballs
Fleischsalat meat salad
Fondue dish of melted cheese to dip bread in, or hot oil to cook meat in
Forelle trout

Frikadelle meatball

Früchte der Saison seasonal fruit

Gans goose

Gänsebraten roast goose

Geflügel poultry

Geflügelsalat chicken salad

Gefüllte Kalbshaxe stuffed veal shanks

Gefüllte Tomaten stuffed tomatoes

Gefüllter Krautkopf stuffed cabbage

Gemischter Salat mixed salad

Gemüse und Beilagen vegetables and side dishes

Gemüsesuppe vegetable soup

Geschmorte Rindsleber braised liver

Götterspeise jelly

Grieß semolina

Grüne Bohnen green beans

Grüner Salat lettuce/green salad

Gulasch mit Nudeln goulash with pasta

Gurkensalat cucumber salad

Hackbraten meatloaf

Hackfleisch mince

Hähnchen chicken

Hähnchen mit Reis chicken with rice

Hamburger Aalsuppe eel soup from Hamburg

Handkäs country cheese

Hase hare

Hasenpfeffer hare or rabbit stew

Heilbutt halibut

Hering herring

Himmel und Erde bacon and meat casserole with apple sauce

Holländische Soße hollandaise sauce

Hummer lobster

Kabeljau cod

Kaiserschmarren sugared, cut up pancakes with raisins

Kalbfleisch veal

Kalbsbraten mit Champignons roast veal with mushrooms

Kalbsfrikassee veal stew

Kalbshaxe knuckle of veal

Kalbsschnitzel cordon bleu veal cutlet with ham and cheese

Karotten carrots

Karpfen carp

Kartoffelbrei mashed potatoes

Kartoffeln potatoes

Kartoffelpuffer potato pancake

Kartoffelsalat potato salad
Kartoffelsuppe potato soup
Käsespätzle cheese noodles
Käseteller cheese platter
Kassler smoked loin of pork
Klöße dumplings
Knoblauch garlic
Knoblauchbrot garlic bread
Knödel dumplings
Kohl cabbage
Kohlrabi kohlrabi (type of cabbage)
Kohlroulade cabbage stuffed with minced meat
Kompott stewed fruit
Königsberger Klopse meatballs in white caper sauce
Kopfsalat lettuce
Kotelett pork chop
Kotelett mit Bratkartoffeln pork chop with fried potatoes
Krabben prawns
Kraftbrühe clear broth
Kräuterbutter herb butter
Krebs crab
Kuchen cakes
Kümmelstangen caraway bread sticks
Kürbis pumpkin
Labskaus thick stew of minced salt meat and herring mixed with mashed potatoes
Lammfleisch lamb
Lammkeule leg of lamb
Lauch leek
Leber liver
Leberkäs meat loaf made with liver
Leberknödel liver dumplings

Leipziger Allerlei Leipzig vegetable platter
Linsensuppe lentil soup
Makrele mackerel
Maluns pasta-filled cabbage
Marinierter Hering pickled herring
Matjeshering salted herring
Maultaschen Swabian ravioli
Maultaschen in Zwiebelsuppe ravioli with onion sauce
Meeresfrüchte seafood
Meerrettichsoße horseradish sauce
Mettwurst smoked sausage spread
Möhren carrots
Muscheln mussels
Nieren kidneys
Nudeln pasta
Nudelsalat pasta salad
Ochsenmaulsalat tongue salad
Oliven olives
Paprika sweet peppers/paprika
Pepperoni hot peppers
Petersiliensoße parsley sauce
Pichelsteiner Eintopf Bavarian stew
Pilze mushrooms
Pizokel tiny, pasta-like dumplings
Pökelfleisch salt meat
Pommes frites chips
Preiselbeeren cranberries
Pumpernickel heavy black bread
Pute turkey
Quark curd cheese
Quarkspeise curd cheese with fruit

Rahmschnitzel cutlet with cream sauce

Rehrücken saddle of venison

Reibekuchen potato pancakes

Reis rice

Rinderbraten roast beef

Rinderschmorbraten in Bier rump of beef in beer

Rindersteak mit Pommes frites steak with chips

Rollmops pickled herring wrapped round slices of onion

Rosenkohl Brussels sprouts

Rösti potato pancakes

Rotkohl red cabbage

Rotkrautsalat red cabbage salad

Roulade slice of rolled beef in gravy

Salate salads

Salatteller salad platter

(Rheinischer) Sauerbraten (Rhineland-style) marinated, braised beef

Sauerkraut pickled white cabbage

Schaschlik-Spieß German-style kebabs

Schinken in Burgunder ham in burgundy sauce

Schmalz goose fat

Schnecken snails

Schnitzel veal or pork cutlet

Schwammerln mushrooms

Schwarzwälder Rehrücken saddle of venison Black Forest style

Schwarzwurzel black salsifies

Schweinebraten roast pork

Schweinebraten mit Kartoffeln oder Klößen roast pork with potatoes or potato dumplings

Seezunge sole

Schnuten und Poten pickled pork and sauerkraut

Spargel asparagus

Spätzle Swabian pasta

Speckkartoffeln potatoes with bacon

Spezialitäten specialities

Spinat spinach

Strammer Max boiled ham and fried eggs served on rye bread

Sülze brawn

Tafelspitz boiled beef

Tunfisch tuna

Tomate tomato

Tomatensalat tomato salad

Weißwurst veal sausage

Wirsing savoy cabbage

Wurst sausage

Zucchini courgettes

Zwiebeln onions

Zwiebelkuchen onion tart

desserts

Apfelkuchen apple cake

Apfelkuchen mit Sahne apple cake with whipped cream

Apfelreis apple rice pudding

Apfelstrudel apple strudel

Berliner doughnut

Bienenstich honey and almond cake

Bremer Klaben a type of sweet bread

Eis ice cream

Eis mit Sahne ice cream with whipped cream

Frankfurter Kranz Frankfurt coffee cake

Haselnusstorte hazelnut gâteau

Käsekuchen cheesecake
Lebkuchen gingerbread
Linzertorte almond flan with raspberry topping
Marmorkuchen marble cake
Mandeltorte almond cake
Mohnkuchen poppy seed cake
Mokka-Nusstorte mocha and nut gâteau
Obsttorte gâteau with fruit topping
Rote Grütze red jelly pudding
Rumtopf rum pot
Pfannkuchen pancake
Pudding blancmange
Sachertorte rich chocolate gâteau
Schlagsahne whipped cream
Schokoladenpudding mit
Schokoladentorte chocolate gâteau

Schwarzwälder Kirschtorte
Black Forest gâteau
Stollen cake with almonds, nuts and dried fruit
Streuselkuchen crumble cake
Torte gâteau
Vanillesoße chocolate pudding with vanilla sauce
Vanilleeis (mit heißen Himbeeren) vanilla ice cream (with hot raspberries)
Zwetschgenkuchen, der plum cake

Entertainment

Germany is a country of major cultural festivals and sporting events. In cities like Berlin and Munich, festival follows festival, but even the smallest and most insignificant towns have full cultural calendars. Ask at the local tourist office for listings of events in English. Berlin, Hamburg and Munich have English-language newspapers and magazines full of dedicated information for visitors.

galleries & museums

Most large towns have an art gallery or local natural history museum. Some of the most unlikely places have some of the most interesting museums – the Herkomer art gallery, for instance, in Landsberg.

cinema

All large cities have cinemas where English-language films can be seen in their original version. There are three major film festivals. In February, the Berlin Film Festival, with its coveted Golden Bear awards, competes with Venice and Cannes; Munich has a lesser-known summer film festival of great charm and without the Cannes glitz. Meanwhile, Saarbrücken's Max Ophüls film festival is a must for aficionados.

folk festivals

Every community has at least two annual festivals, and some have several. Carnival – or **Fasching**, as it's known in the South – is celebrated with gusto in the week leading up to Lent. Summer festivals usually have themes attached to them (the river jousting in Ulm, for instance). Every village boasting a vineyard has an autumn wine festival, while some of the larger ones (Stuttgart, for instance) are staggering affairs. Bavaria's summer festivals are usually centred on beer, climaxing with Munich's famous **Oktoberfest** (which actually begins in September).

music & opera

The Richard Wagner opera festival in Bayreuth is world famous, but there are hundreds of smaller seasons of concert music, opera and ballet offering comparable quality at lower prices. Munich's annual opera festival competes with Bayreuth for star attraction, and there are atmospheric outdoor summer events throughout the country. Every church with an organ has a festival of recitals, usually during the summer months.

sport

Football Berlin, Cologne, Dresden, Frankfurt, Hamburg, Munich and Nuremberg all have premier-league football clubs with impresssive home grounds, where tickets are usually readily available for all but the most hotly contested local derbies. Bayern Munich plays in Munich's Olympic stadium, so a visit to a match there can be combined with a tour of the site.

Tennis Public tennis courts are everywhere. Although there is usually no problem booking a court, it can be quite expensive.

Golf There are still very few public courses and visitors usually need to show a foreign club membership and a handicap in order to play.

Sailing You can rent dinghies and cabin-cruisers on the coast and all the inland lakes. Proof of proficiency is required by most boatyards.

Horseriding There are many pretty bridle paths all over Germany. You might be asked to prove ability before being allowed to go trekking.

Fishing Anglers must obtain a licence in all areas (check at the local tourist office). There are quite severe penalties for poaching.

Hiking There are few restrictions on access to the magnificent walking and mountaineering in the uplands and southern Alps. Climbers should contact local clubs (through regional tourist offices) before tackling high peaks.

Cycling Mountain bikes can be hired at every Alpine resort, and in most towns, often at railway stations or hotels. Cyclists are privileged road-users in most German cities, and there is no shortage of cycle paths.

Winter sports Germany offers both cross-country and alpine skiing. Garmisch-Partenkirchen, the venue for the 1936 Winter Olympics, is the country's top ski resort, with year-round glacier skiing on the Zugspitze (Germany's highest peak, at 9,731ft). There are many more well-known resorts along the mountain ranges which mark Germany's southern border.

The ski resorts are also very popular summer-time destinations. The thick fir forests offer shady walking, and the mountain lakes are warm enough to swim in.

children

Germany has several theme parks to keep children entertained. The Haßloch Holidaypark is located on Germany's 'Wine Route' between Neustadt and Speyer, and the Europapark is in Rust, near Freiburg. Also worth a visit are the Freizeitpark Tripsdrill, twelve miles south of Heilbronn, Wiesbaden's Taunus Wonderland and the leisure parks at Steinau an der Straße (a must for those in search of the roots of the Grimm fairy tales) and Ziegenhagen (between Göttingen and Kassel).

Entertainment

phrasemaker

finding out what's on
you may say …

Do you have …	Haben Sie …	*haaben zee*
an entertainment guide?	einen Veranstalt- ungskalender?	*iynen feranshtalt- oongskalender*
a map of the town?	einen Stadtplan?	*iynen shtatplaan*
Do you have it in English?	Haben Sie das auf Englisch?	*haaben zee das owf english*
What is there to do/see here?	Was gibt es hier zu tun/sehen?	*vas geept es heer tsooh toohn/zayen*
Is there anything for children to do?	Gibt es hier etwas für Kinder?	*geept es heer etvas fewr kinder*
Is there …	Gibt es …	*geept es*
a guided tour?	eine Führung?	*iyne fewroong*
a bus tour?	eine Stadtrundfahrt?	*iyne shtatroontfaart*
a tourist office?	eine Touristen- information?	*iyne tooristen- informatsyohn*
a cinema?	ein Kino?	*iyn keeno*
a swimming pool?	ein Schwimmbad?	*iyn shvimmbaat*
a golf course?	einen Golfplatz?	*iynen golfplats*
Where is … please?	Wo ist …, bitte?	*voh ist … bitte*
the (art) gallery	die (Kunst)galerie	*dee (koonst)galeree*
the castle	das Schloss	*das shloss*
the church	die Kirche	*dee keershe*
the theatre	das Theater	*das tayaater*
We'd like to do a trip.	Wir möchten eine Fahrt machen.	*veer mershten iyne faart maken*
Are there any … here?	Gibt es … hier?	*geept es … heer*
nightclubs	Nachtklubs	*naktklups*
parks	Parks	*parks*
Can you recommend …	Können Sie … empfehlen?	*kernnen zee empfaylen*
a museum?	ein Museum?	*iyn moozayoom*
an exhibition?	eine Ausstellung	*iyne owsshtelloong*

you may hear …

Wofür interessieren Sie sich?	*voh*fewr interes*see*ren zee zish	What are you interested in?
Es gibt eine Führung.	es geept *iy*ne *few*roong	There's a guided tour.
Der Bus fährt …	der boos fayrt	The bus leaves …
jede Stunde.	*yay*de *shtoon*de	every hour.
zur vollen Stunde.	tsoohr *fo*llen *shtoon*de	on the hour.
alle zwei Stunden.	alle tsviy *shtoon*den	every two hours.
Das Museum ist …	das moo*zay*oom ist	The museum is …
am Marktplatz.	am *markt*plats	in the market square.
im Zentrum.	im *tsent*room	in the centre.
in der Bahnhofstraße.	in der *baan*hohfshtraasse	on Station Street.
Es gibt zwei …	es geept tsviy	There are two …
Theater.	tay*aa*ter	theatres.
Stadien.	*shtaa*dyen	stadiums.

Entertainment

getting more information
you may say ...

When does it start?	Wann fängt es an?	*vann fengt es an*
When does ... finish?	Wann ist ... zu Ende?	*vann ist ... tsooh ende*
it	es	*es*
the performance	die Vorstellung	*dee fohrshtelloong*
the musical	das Musical	*das mewzikal*
the opera	die Oper	*dee ohper*
the fair	die Messe	*dee messe*
the concert	das Konzert	*das kontsert*
the fireworks	das Feuerwerk	*das foyervayrk*
How long is ...	Wie lange dauert ...	*vee lange dowert*
the tour?	die Fahrt?	*dee faart*
the film?	der Film?	*der film*
the sightseeing tour?	die Besichtigung?	*dee bezishtigoong*
the (football) match?	das (Fußball)spiel?	*das (foohssball)shpeel*
Will there be an interval?	Gibt es eine Pause?	*geept es iyne powze*
Where do I get the tickets?	Wo bekomme ich die Karten, bitte?	*voh bekomme ish dee karten bitte*
Do you need tickets?	Braucht man Eintrittskarten?	*browkt man iyntrittskarten*
What are the opening hours?	Wie sind die Öffnungszeiten?	*vee zint dee erffnoongstsiyten*
Is it open ...	Ist es ... geöffnet?	*ist es ... geerffnet*
on Mondays?	montags	*mohntaaks*
at the weekend?	am Wochenende	*am vokenende*
Is there wheelchair access?	Gibt es einen Rollstuhlzugang?	*geept es iynen rollshtoohltsoohgang*
Is it also in English?	Ist es auch auf Englisch?	*ist es owk owf english*
Does the film have subtitles?	Hat der Film Untertitel?	*hat der film oontertitel*
Where does the bus leave from?	Wo fährt der Bus ab?	*voh fayrt der boos ap*

you may hear ...

Es ist ... geschlossen.	es ist ... geshlossen	It is closed ...
sonntags	zonntaaks	on Sundays.
im Winter	im vinter	in the winter.
Die Vorstellung ...	dee fohrshtelloong	The performance ...
fängt um sieben Uhr an.	fengt oom zeeben an	starts at 7pm.
dauert bis zehn Uhr.	dowert bis tsayn oohr	finishes at 10pm.
dauert zwei Stunden.	dowert tsviy shtoonden	lasts two hours.
Sie können die Karten ... kaufen.	zee kernnen dee karten ... kowfen	You can buy the tickets ...
hier	heer	here.
am Schalter	am shalter	at the counter.
Die Pause ist zwanzig Minuten.	dee powze ist tsvantsik minoohten	The interval is 20 minutes.
Der Bus fährt vom Hauptbahnhof ab.	der boos fayrt fom ap howptbaanhohf	The bus leaves from the main station.

check out 1

At the tourist office, you ask about the national gallery.

○ Entschuldigung, wo ist die Nationalgalerie?
  entshooldigoong voh ist dee natsyonaalgaleree

- Sie ist am Bahnhof, in der Ottostraße.
  zee ist am baanhohf in der ottoshtraasse

○ Wie sind die Öffnungszeiten?
  vee zint dee erffnoongstsiyten

- Von neun bis sechzehn Uhr.
  fon noyn bis zeshtsayn oohr

○ Danke schön.
  danke shern

Q Where is the gallery?
What are the opening hours?

Entertainment

buying a ticket

you may say ...

How much is it?	Was kostet das?	vas **kost**et das
How much are tickets for ...	Was kosten die Karten für ...	vas **kos**ten dee **kar**ten fewr
adults?	Erwachsene?	er**vak**sene
children?	Kinder?	**kin**der
Is there a concession for ...	Gibt es Ermäßigung für ...	**geept** es er**may**ssigoong fewr
students?	Studenten?	shtoo**den**ten
pensioners?	Rentner?	**rent**ner
people with disabilities?	Behinderte?	be**hin**derte
What seats do you have left?	Was für Plätze haben Sie noch?	vas fewr **plet**se **haa**ben zee nok
Are the seats numbered?	Sind die Plätze nummeriert?	zint dee **plet**se noomme**reert**
Is this seat available?	Ist dieser Platz noch frei?	ist **dee**zer plats nok friy
Where can I buy a programme?	Wo kann ich ein Programm kaufen?	voh kann ish iyn pro**gramm kow**fen

you may hear ...

Er ist frei/besetzt.	er ist friy/be**zetst**	It is available/taken.
Wir haben noch Plätze ...	veer **haa**ben nok **plet**se	We have got seats ...
im Parkett.	im par**kett**	in the stalls.
im Rang.	im	in the circle.
in der Loge.	in der **loh**she	in the boxes.
Wir sind heute leider ausverkauft.	veer zint **hoy**te **liy**der **ows**ferkowft	I am sorry, we are sold out tonight.
Sie können sitzen, wo Sie möchten.	zee **kern**nen **zit**sen voh zee **mersh**ten	You can sit where you like.
Eine Karte/Familienkarte kostet zehn Euro.	**iy**ne **kar**te/ fa**meely**enkarte **kos**tet tsayn **oy**ro	A ticket/family ticket is €10.
hier/dort drüben	heer/dort **drew**ben	here/over there

check out 2

You are asking about a performance of Aida.

○ Was kosten die Karten für Aida?
*vas **kos**ten dee **kar**ten fewr a-**ee**da*

- Zweiundsechzig Euro.
tsviyoontzeshtsig oyro

○ Wie lange dauert die Vorstellung?
*vee **lan**ge **dow**ert dee **fohr**shtelloong*

- Vier Stunden. Sie fängt um sechs Uhr an und dauert
bis zehn Uhr.
*feer **shtoon**den. zee fengt oom zeks oohr an oont **dow**ert
bis tsayn oohr*

Q How much are tickets?
How long does the opera last?

signs

you may see …

Ausgang	exit
Bar	bar
Galerie	balcony
Garderobe	cloakroom
Notausgang	emergency exit
Parkett	stall
Rang	circle
Toiletten	toilets
Damen/Herren	Ladies/Gents
Treppe	stairs

swimming & sunbathing

you may say …

Where can I …	Wo kann ich …	*voh kann ish*
go swimming?	schwimmen gehen?	*shvimmen gayen*
Can I use the hotel pool?	Kann ich das Hotelschwimmbad benutzen?	*kann ish das hotelshvimmbaat benootsen*
Where are … please?	Wo sind die …, bitte?	*voh zint dee … bitte*
the changing rooms	Umkleidekabinen	*oomkliydekabeenen*
the hairdryers	Haartrockener	*haartrokner*
the showers	Duschen	*dooshen*
the lockers	Schließfächer	*shleessfesher*
Do I need …	Brauche ich …	*browke ish*
change?	Kleingeld?	*klyingelt*
a swimming cap?	eine Badekappe?	*iyne baadekappe*
Is it okay to swim here?	Kann man hier schwimmen?	*kann man heer shvimmen*
Is it dangerous?	Ist es gefährlich?	*ist es gefayrlish*
I'd like to hire …	Ich möchte … leihen.	*ish mershte … layen*
a parasol.	einen Sonnenschirm	*iynen zonnenshirm*
a deck chair.	einen Liegestuhl	*iynen leegeshtoohl*
a sun lounger.	eine Sonnenliege	*iyne sonnenleege*
a beach towel.	ein Badetuch	*iyn baadetoohk*
How long can I stay in the pool?	Wie lange kann ich im Bad bleiben?	*vee lange kann ish im baat bliyben*
I'd like some …	Ich möchte …	*ish mershte*
sunglasses.	eine Sonnenbrille.	*iyne zonnenbrille*
sun cream.	einen Sonnenscreme.	*iynen zonnenkraym*

signs
you may see ...

20m tief	20m deep
die Ebbe/die Flut	low/high tide
erste Hilfe	first aid
Rettungsschwimmer	lifeguard
starke Strömung	strong current

check out 3

You arrive at the swimming pool.

○ Guten Tag. Zwei Erwachsene, bitte.
 goohten taak. tsviy ervaksene bitte

- Fünf Euro zwanzig, bitte.
 fewnf oyro tsvantsig bitte

○ Wie lange kann ich im Bad bleiben?
 vee lange kann ish im baat bliyben

- Zwei Stunden.
 tsviy shtoonden

○ Und wo sind die Umkleidekabinen?
 oont voh zint dee oomkliydekabeenen

Q How much is a ticket?
You ask where the lockers are: true or false?

sports
you may say ...

Where can I ... play tennis/golf/ volleyball? go walking? go mountain- biking?	Wo kann ich ... Tennis/Golf/ Volleyball spielen? wandern? Mountainbike fahren?	*voh kann ish* *tennis/golf/* *vollayball shpeelen* *vandern* *mowntenbiyk faaren*
I'd like to hire ... a racket. a bike. waterskis.	Ich möchte ... leihen. einen Schläger ein Fahrrad Wasserskier	*ish mershte ... liyen* *iynen shlayger* *iyn faarrat* *vassersheeer*
I'd like to take ... lessons. skiing sailing horseriding	Ich möchte ... nehmen. Skiunterricht Segelunterricht Reitunterricht	*ish mershte ...* *naymen* *sheeoonterrisht* *zaygeloonterrisht* *riytoonterrisht*
How much is it per hour/per day?	Was kostet das pro Stunde/pro Tag?	*vas kostet das proh* *shtoonde/proh taak*
Can children do it too?	Sind Kinder erlaubt?	*zint kinder erlowpt*
climbing	das Bergsteigen	*das bayrkshtiygen*
surfing	das Surfen	*das serfen*
windsurfing	das Windsurfen	*das vintserfen*
diving	das Tauchen	*das towken*

you may hear ...

Das kostet zwanzig Euro pro Stunde/Tag.	*das kostet tsvantsig* *oyro proh shtoonde/* *taak*	It's €20 per hour/ day.
Ja, das bekommen Sie hier.	*yaa, das bekommen* *zee heer*	Yes, you get it here.

sports equipment

balls	die Bälle	dee *be*lle
boots	die Stiefel	dee *shtee*fel
golf clubs	die Golfschläger	dee *golf*shlayger
inline skates	die Inline-Skates	dee *in*liynskayts
sailing boat	das Segelboot	das *zay*gelboht
surfboard	das Surfbrett	das *serf*brett
waterskis	die Wasserskier	dee *va*ssershee-er

check out 4

At the beach, you fancy trying some of the water sports on offer.

○ Ich möchte Windsurf-Unterricht nehmen.
  ish mershte vintserf oonterrisht naymen

- Heute oder morgen?
  hoyte ohder morgen

○ Heute. Was kostet das pro Stunde?
  hoyte. vas kostet das proh shtoonde

- Das kostet fünfzehn Euro pro Stunde.
  das kostet fewnftsayn oyro proh shtoonde

○ Sind Kinder erlaubt?
  zint kinder erlowpt

- Leider nicht. Es ist zu gefährlich.
  liyder nisht. es ist tsooh gefayrlish

Q What kind of lessons do you want to take?
Is your son allowed to do it as well?

winter sports

downhill skiing	der Abfahrtslauf	der **ap**faartslowf
cross-country skiing	der Skilanglauf	der **shee**langlowf
snowboarding	das Snowboarden	das **snoh**borhden
ice-skating	das Eislaufen	das **iys**lowfen
cable car	die seilbahn	dee **ziyl**baan
ski boots	die Skistiefel	dee **shee**shteefel
chair lift	der Sessellift	der **ze**ssellift
ski pass	der Skipass	der **shee**pass
ski run	die Skipiste	dee **shee**pisste
drag lift	der Schlepplift	der **shlepp**lift
skis	die Skier	dee **shee**-er
snowboard	das Snowboard	das **snoh**bohrd
toboggan	der Schlitten	der **shli**tten
skates	die Schlittschuhe	dee **shlitt**shoohe

sound check

st has the same pronunciation as in English if it's in the middle of a word:

kosten *kosten*   Gast *gast*

At the beginning of a word, however, it is pronounced 'sht':

Stadtrundfahrt *shtatroontfaart*   Stunde *shtoonde*

This rule still applies when two words are combined:

Skisstiefel *sheeshteefel*   liegestuhl *leegeshtoohl*

Or when prepositions like **vor** and **aus** are part of a word:

Vorstellung *fohrshtelloong*   Austellung *owsshtelloong*

try it out

in the mix

Here are six places you might want to visit. Can you unscramble them?

1 ausllestung   **4** clbunacht

2 noki   **5** shcwimmbda

3 eaterth   **6** tenspielnis

as if you were there

You want to join a bus tour of Cologne. Follow the prompts to play your part.

(Ask where the bus leaves from)
Um elf Uhr, vom Hauptbahnhof.
(Ask how long the tour takes)
Drei Stunden mit Pause.
(Ask where you can buy tickets)
Sie können die Karten hier kaufen.

Entertainment

linkup

key phrases

Wo ist das Stadion?	**Where is** the stadium?
Was kosten die Karten?	**How much are** the tickets?
Gibt es hier Nachtklubs?	**Arethere** any nightclubs **here**?
Wie lange dauert die Fahrt?	**How long does** the trip **take**?
Wo kann ich schwimmen gehen?	**Where can I** go swimming?
Wann beginnt der Film?	**What time** does the film **start**?

telling the time

If you want to say what time something happens, you can often say it as you would in English:

Die Oper beginnt um neun (Uhr). The opera begins at nine (o'clock).

In informal speech, the word Uhr can be left out, but only for numbers one to twelve. Other phrases for telling the time are:

viertel nach neun a quarter past nine

viertel vor neun a quarter to nine

halb neun half past eight

Note that halb neun does not mean 'half past nine' but 'half past eight' as it refers to the fact that you are only halfway through the ninth hour.

In formal language, Germans use the 24 hour clock:

Das Konzert endet um 22 Uhr. The concert finishes at 10pm.

Der Zug fährt um 14:35 Uhr (14 Uhr 35) ab. The train leaves at 2.35pm.

Emergencies

reporting crime

Report all incidents immediately to the **Polizei** (police). German police are generally very helpful and they all speak some English. (English is the primary foreign language taught in German secondary schools.)

It is considered an offence not to carry any form of identification, so it is a good idea to keep your passport with you at all times – a drivers' licence will do just as well. If the police want to stop you while you are driving, they will switch on a sign saying **Polizei, bitte anhalten**. Stay calm and follow their instructions but if you respect the speed limits there is no reason that you should be stopped at all.

accidents & illness

The **Unfallstation** (casualty department) of the local **Krankenhaus** (hospital) should be able to deal with most accidents and other medical emergencies.

To call a **Krankenwagen** (ambulance) dial 112. Legally, they must respond to every call, regardless of insurance issues.

EU nationals need a valid European Health Insurance Card to be entitled to free or reduced-cost medical care while in Germany. They are available from UK post offices, or online: **www.dh.gov.uk/travellers**.

For less urgent cases, an **Apotheke** (chemist's – look for the large red A sign) can dispense **rezeptpflichtige Medikamente** (prescription medicines), over-the-counter medicine and advice, often in English. They may also be able to recommend a doctor. Don't confuse this with a **Drogerie**, which sells toiletries, cosmetics and health food.

car breakdown

Arrows on posts along the **Autobahn** (motorway) guide you to the next emergency phone (every mile or so). On other roads, call directory

enquiries (11833) from the nearest phone for the numbers of local **Pannendienste** (recovery services). Contact your hirer or insurer to find out if they have a reciprocal agreement with a German company.

travellers with disabilities

Germany generally caters well for disabled travellers. Most public places are wheelchair-accessible. Public transport also tends to cater for wheelchair users and many hotels offer wheelchair-friendly rooms. Under the slogan 'Tourism without Barriers', the DZT (**Deutsche Zentrale für Tourismus**) offers holidaymakers with restricted mobility a wide range of travel options and packages that include accommodation, activities and services for disabled people. See: **www.germany-tourism.de**.

post offices

Postämter (post offices) tend to keep the same opening hours as shops, with an hour lunch break. Stamps must be bought here.

phone calls

If using a public phone, you'll need a **Telefonkarte** (phone card), available for €5 or €10 from post offices or news kiosks. Many public phones now take Visa or Master/Eurocard.

Emergencies 112
Ambulance 112
Police 110
Fire 112
Directory enquiries 11833

phrasemaker

emergency phrases
you may say …

Can you help me?	Können Sie mir helfen?	*kernnen zee meer helfen*
Excuse me!	Entschuldigung!	*entshooldigoong*
Hello there!	Hallo!	*hallo*
Help!	Hilfe!	*hilfe*
I'll call the police!	Ich rufe die Polizei!	*ish roohfe dee politsiy*
It's urgent!	Es ist dringend!	*es ist dringent*
Leave me alone!	Lass mich in Ruhe!	*lass mish in roohe*
Is there someone here who speaks English?	Spricht hier jemand Englisch?	*shprisht heer yaymant english*
Thank you!	Danke schön!	*danke shern*
Where is the nearest …	Wo ist die nächste …	*voh ist dee naykste*
chemist's?	Apotheke?	*apotayke*
casualty department?	Unfallstation?	*oohnfallshtatsyohn*
garage?	Autowerkstatt?	*owtovayrkshtatt*
petrol station?	Tankstelle?	*tankshtelle*
police station?	Polizeiwache?	*politsiyvake*
Where is the nearest …	Wo ist das nächste …	*voh ist das naykste*
hospital?	Krankenhaus?	*krankenhows*
lost property?	Fundbüro?	*foontbewro*
telephone?	Telefon?	*telayfon*
I need …	Ich brauche …	*ish browke*
a doctor.	einen Arzt.	*iynen aartst*
an ambulance.	einen Krankenwagen.	*iynen krankenvaagen*

telling the doctor or dentist

you may say ...

I'd like an appointment with a doctor/a dentist.	Ich möchte einen Arzttermin/ Zahnarzttermin- machen.	*ish **mershte iy**nen **aartst**termeen/ **tsaan**aartsttermeen **ma**ken*
My ... hurts.	Mein ... tut weh.	*miyn ... tooht vay*
head	Kopf	*kopf*
tooth	Zahn	*tsaan*
throat	Hals	*hals*
It hurts here.	Es tut hier weh.	*es tooht heer vay*
I'm in a lot of pain.	Ich habe starke Schmerzen.	*ish **haa**be **shtaar**ke **shmer**tsen*
I can't move/feel ...	Ich kann ... nicht bewegen/fühlen.	*ish kann ... nisht be**vay**gen/**few**len*
my neck.	mein Genick	*miyn ge**nik***
my leg.	mein Bein	*miyn biyn*
I've ... myself.	Ich habe mich ...	*ish **haa**be mish*
cut	geschnitten.	*ge**shnit**ten*
burnt	verbrannt.	*fer**brannt***
I feel ...	Mir ist ...	*meer ist*
sick.	schlecht.	*shlesht*
dizzy.	schwindlig.	***shvin**dlig*
I've been bitten by a dog.	Ein Hund hat mich gebissen.	*iyn hoont hat mish ge**bis**sen*
I've been bitten by an insect.	Ein Insekt hat mich gestochen.	*iyn in**zekt** hat mish ge**shto**ken*
I've been sick.	Ich habe mich übergeben.	*ish **haa**be mish ewber**gay**ben*
I'm allergic to ...	Ich bin gegen ... allergisch.	*ish bin **gay**gen ... al**layr**gish*
antibiotics.	Antibiotika	*anti**byoh**tika*
animals.	Tiere	***tee**re*
I'm ...	Ich bin ...	*ish bin*
diabetic.	Diabetiker/in.	*deea**bay**tiker/in*
pregnant.	schwanger.	***shvan**ger*
epileptic.	Epileptiker/in.	*epi**lep**tiker/in*
HIV positive.	HIV-positiv.	*haa-ee-**fow poh**ziteef*

I have ...	Ich habe ...	*ish haabe*
asthma.	Asthma.	*astma*
high/low blood pressure.	hohen/niedrigen Blutdruck.	*hohen/needrigen bloohtdrook*
I have a heart condition.	Ich bin herzkrank.	*ish bin hertskrank*
I've lost a filling.	Ich habe eine Plombe verloren.	*ish haabe iyne plombe ferlohren*
Could you give me a prescription?	Können Sie mir ein Rezept geben?	*kernnen zee meer iyn retsept gayben*
Could you transfer me to a specialist?	Können Sie mich an einen Spezialisten überweisen?	*kernnen zee mish an iynen shpaytsyalisten ewberviyzen*

you may hear ...

Wie geht es Ihnen?	*vee gayt es eenen*	How are you?
Wo tut es weh?	*voh tooht es vay*	Where does it hurt?
Machen Sie sich bitte frei.	*maken zee zish bitte friy*	Please undress.
Nehmen Sie Medizin ein?	*naymen zee meditseen iyn*	Are you on medication?
Haben Sie irgendwelche Allergien?	*haaben zee irgentvelshe allergeen*	Are you allergic to anything?
Ich muss Sie untersuchen.	*ish mooss zee oonterzoohken*	I have to examine you.
Haben Sie eine Europäische Krankenver-sicherungskarte?	*haaben zee iyne oyropayishe krankenferzisheroongs-karte*	Do you have an EHIC?
Es ist nicht schlimm.	*es ist nisht shlimm*	It is not serious.
Es ist ...	*es ist*	It's ...
gebrochen.	*gebroken*	a fracture.
eine Muskelzerrung.	*iyne mooskeltserroong*	a pulled muscle.
eine Lebensmit-telvergiftung.	*iyne laybensmittelfer-giftoong*	food poisoning.

Der Knochen ist gebrochen.	*der knoken ist gebroken*	The bone is broken.
Sie müssen ...	*zee mewssen*	You need ...
operiert werden.	*opereert vayrden*	an operation.
geröntgt werden.	*gerernsht vayrden*	an X-ray.
Ich mache Ihnen eine Plombe.	*ish make eenen iyne plombe*	I'll put in a filling.
Ich muss den Zahn ziehen.	*ish mooss dayn tsaan tseeyen*	I'll have to take this tooth out.
Sie müssen ...	*zee mewssen*	You must ...
im Bett bleiben.	*im bett bliyben*	stay in bed.
sich ausruhen.	*zish owsroohen*	rest.
viel Wasser trinken.	*feel vasser trinken*	drink lots of water.
Sie dürfen nicht ...	*zee dewrfen nisht*	You mustn't ...
aufstehen.	*owfshtayen*	get up.
rennen.	*rennen*	run.
Sport treiben.	*shport triyben*	take exercise.

at the chemist's

you may say ...

Have you got anything for ...	Haben Sie etwas gegen ...	*haaben zee etvas gaygen*
a headache?	Kopfschmerzen?	*kopfshmertsen*
hayfever?	Heuschnupfen?	*hoyshnoopfen*
stomach ache?	Magenschmerzen?	*maagenshmertsen*
indigestion?	Verdauungsbeschwerden?	*ferdowoongsbeshvayrden*
nausea?	Übelkeit?	*ewbelkiyt*
insomnia?	Schlaflosigkeit?	*shlaaflohzigkiyt*
constipation?	Verstopfung?	*fershtopfoong*
insect bites?	Insektensstiche?	*inzektenshtishe*
travel sickness?	Reisekrankheit?	*riyzekrankhiyt*

I've got ...	Ich habe ...	*ish haabe*
a cold.	eine Erkältung.	*iyne erkeltoong*
a cough.	Husten.	*hoosten*
a fever.	Fieber.	*feeber*
'flu.	Grippe.	*grippe*

Can you recommend anything?	Können Sie etwas empfehlen?	*kernnen zee etvas empfaylen*
Is it a strong medicine?	Ist das Medikament stark?	*ist das medikament shtaark*
Does it contain penicillin?	Enthält es Penizillin?	*enthelt es penitsileen*
How often do I have to take it?	Wie oft muss ich das nehmen?	*vee oft mooss ish das naymen*
Does it have side effects?	Hat es Nebenwirkungen?	*hat es naybenvirkoongen*
Do I need a prescription?	Brauche ich ein Rezept?	*browke ish iyn retsept*

you may hear ...

Nehmen Sie das einmal/zweimal/ dreimal täglich.	*naymen zee das iynmaal/tsviymaal/ driymaal tayklish*	Take this once/twice/ three times a day.
mit Wasser	*mit vasser*	with water

Möchten Sie ...	*mershten zee*	Would you like ...
Tabletten?	*tabletten*	tablets?
Creme?	*kraym*	cream?
Saft?	*zaft*	liquid?
Tropfen?	*tropfen*	drops?
eine kleine/große Packung/Flasche?	*iyne kliyne/grohsse pakoon/flashe*	a small/big packet/ bottle?
morgens/mittags/ abends	*morgens/mittaags/ aabents*	in the morning/at lunchtime/in the evening
vor/nach dem Essen	*fohr/naak daym essen*	before/after the meal
Kann Müdigkeit hervorrufen.	*kann mewdigkiyt herfohrroohfen*	May cause drowsiness.
Ganz schlucken.	*gants shlooken*	Swallow whole.
Kauen, nicht schlucken.	*kowen nisht shlooken*	Chew, do not swallow whole.
Kontakt mit Augen vermeiden.	*kontakt mit owgen fermiyden*	Avoid contact with your eyes.
Das ist rezeptpflichtig.	*das ist retseptpflishtig*	You need a prescription for that.
Was haben Sie gegessen/getrunken?	*vas haaben zee gegessen/getroonken*	What have you eaten/drunk?

toiletries

after-sun lotion	After-Sun-Lotion	*aafter-san-lotsyohn*
condoms	Kondome	*kondohme*
cough medicine	Hustenmedizin	*hoostenmayditseen*
insect repellent	ein Insektenschutz- mittel	*iyn inzektenshoots- mittel*
nappies	Windeln	*vindeln*
painkillers	Schmerztabletten	*shmertstabletten*
plasters	die Pflaster	*dee pflaster*
sanitary towels	die Damenbinden	*dee daamenbinden*
shampoo	Shampoo	*shampooh*
sun lotion	Sonnencreme	*zonnenkraym*
tampons	die Tampons	*dee tampons*
toothbrush	eine Zahnbürste	*iyne tsaanbewrste*
toothpaste	Zahnpasta	*tsaanpasta*

parts of the body

ankle	der Fußknöchel	*der foohssknershel*
arm	der Arm	*der aarm*
back	der Rücken	*der rewken*
chest	die Brust	*dee broost*
ear	das Ohr	*das ohr*
eyes	die Augen	*dee owgen*
fingers	die Finger	*dee finger*
head	der Kopf	*der kopf*
hip	die Hüfte	*dee hewfte*
knee	das Knie	*das knee*
leg	das Bein	*das biyn*
neck	das Genick	*das genik*
shoulder	die Schulter	*dee shoolter*
stomach	der Magen	*der maagen*
tooth/teeth	der Zahn/die Zähne	*der tsaan/dee tsayne*

check out 1

You're at the chemist's to buy some tablets for a headache.

○ Entschuldigung, ich brauche Kopfschmerztabletten. Können Sie etwas empfehlen?
entshooldigoong ish browke kopfshmertstabletten. kernnen zee etvas empfaylen

- Diese Tabletten sind gut. Möchten Sie eine große oder eine kleine Packung?
deeze tabletten zint gooht. mershten zee iyne grohsse ohder iyne kliyne pakoong

○ Eine große, bitte.
iyne grohsse bitte

(gut = good)

Q What choice does the chemist offer you?

Emergencies

check out 2

You're feeling sick, and make an appointment to see a doctor.

○ Wie geht es Ihnen?
vee gayt es eenen

- Mir ist schlecht.
meer ist shlesht

○ Was haben Sie gegessen?
vas haaben zee gegessen

- Muscheln, gestern Abend. Können Sie mir ein Rezept geben?
moosheln gestern aabent. kernnen zee meer iyn retsept gayben

○ Natürlich. Haben Sie eine Europäische Krankenversicherungskarte?
natewrlish. haaben zee iyne oyropayishe krankenferzisheroongskarte

Q The doctor asks what you've drunk: true or false?
Will the doctor give you a prescription?

at the police station

you may say …

I've lost …	Ich habe … verloren.	*ish haabe … ferlohren*
my passport.	meinen Pass	*miynen pass*
my luggage.	mein Gepäck	*miyn gepek*
my wallet.	meine Brieftasche	*miyne breeftashe*
my son/daughter.	meinen Sohn/meine Tochter	*miynen zohn/miyne tokter*
My … was stolen.	Mein … wurde gestohlen.	*miyn … voorde geshtohlen*
suitcase	Koffer	*koffer*
car	Auto	*owto*
money	Geld	*gelt*

Our car has been broken into.	Unser Auto ist aufgebrochen worden.	*oonzer owto ist owfgebroken vorden*
I was mugged.	Ich bin überfallen worden.	*ish bin ewberfallen vorden*
I had an accident.	Ich hatte einen Unfall.	*ish hatte iynen oohnfall*
yesterday ... morning afternoon evening	gestern ... Morgen Nachmittag Abend	*gestern* *morgen* *nakmittaak* *aabent*
this morning	heute Morgen	*hoyte morgen*
in a shop/the street	im Geschäft/auf der Straße	*im gesheft/owf der shtraasse*
It's ... big. blue. expensive. made of leather.	Es ist ... groß. blau. teuer. aus Leder.	*es ist* *grohss* *blow* *toyer* *ows layder*
Was ... handed in?	Ist ... abgegeben worden?	*ist ... apgegayben vorden*

Emergencies

you may hear ...

Was ist passiert?	*vas ist passeert*	What happened?
Wann/Wo ist das passiert?	*vann/voh ist das passeert*	When/Where did that happen?
Sind Sie verletzt?	*zint zee ferletst*	Are you hurt?
Wie ist ... Ihr Name? Ihre Adresse?	*vee ist eer naame eere adresse*	What's your ... name? address?
Wie heißt Ihr Hotel?	*vee hiysst eer hotel*	What's the name of your hotel?
Haben Sie einen Ausweis dabei?	*haaben zee iynen owsviys dabiy*	Have you got any ID on you?
Bitte füllen Sie das Formular aus.	*bitte fewllen zee das formulaar ows*	Please fill in this form.
Wie sieht ... aus?	*vee zeet ... ows*	What does ... look like?
Ja, Sie haben Glück.	*yaa zee haaben glewk*	Yes, you're in luck.
Hier ist nichts abgegeben worden.	*heer ist nishts apgegayben vorden*	Nothing has been handed in.

check out 3

You go to the police station to report a theft.

○ Guten Tag, mein Geld wurde gestohlen.
  goohten taak miyn gelt voorde geshtohlen

- Wo ist das passiert?
  voh ist das passeert

○ Im Hotel.
  im hotel

- Wie heißt Ihr Hotel?
  vee hiysst eer hotel

○ Hotel zur Post.
  hotel tsoor post

Q What was stolen?
Where did the theft take place?

valuables

briefcase	der Aktenkoffer	*der **akten**koffer*
digital camera	die Digitalkamera	*dee digi**taal**kamera*
driving licence	der Führerschein	*der **few**rershiyn*
handbag	die Handtasche	*dee **hant**tashe*
jewellery	der Schmuck	*der **shmook***
laptop	der Laptop	*der **lep**top*
mobile	das Handy	*das **hen**dee*
mp3 player	der MP3-Player	*der empay**driy**-player*
necklace	die Kette	*dee **kette***
passport	der Reisepaß	*der **riy**zepass*
purse	das Portemonnaie	*das portmo**nnay***
wallet	die Brieftasche	*dee **breef**tashe*

car breakdown

you may say …

Please could you help me?	Könnten Sie mir bitte helfen?	*kernnten zee meer bitte **hel**fen*
My car has broken down.	Ich habe eine Panne.	*ish **haa**be **iy**ne **panne***
on the motorway A28	auf der Autobahn A28	*owf der **owto**baan aa aktoont**tsvan**tsig*
two kilometres from …	zwei Kilometer von …	*tsviy keelo**may**ter fon*
I need tools.	Ich brauche Werkzeug.	*ish **brow**ke **vayrk**tsoyk*
How far is the next …	Wie weit ist die/der/das nächste …	*vee viyt ist dee/der/das **nayk**ste*

… isn't working.
  The engine
  The steering
	… funktioniert nicht.
	  Der Motor
	  Die Lenkung
		*foonktsyo**neert** nisht
		  der **moh**tor
		  dee **len**koong*

The brakes aren't working.	Die Bremsen funktionieren nicht.	*dee **brem**zen foonktsyo**nee**ren nisht*
I have a puncture.	Ich habe eine Reifenpanne.	*ish **haa**be **iy**ne **riy**fenpanne*

Emergencies

| I've run out of petrol. | Ich habe kein Benzin mehr. | *ish **haa**be kiyn bent**seen** mayr* |
| When will it be ready? | Wann ist es fertig? | *vann ist es **fer**tig* |

Was ist passiert?	*vas ist pa**seert***	What happened?
Wann/Wo …?	*vann/voh*	When/Where …?
Wir schicken einen Mechaniker.	*veer **shik**en **iy**nen me**shaa**niker*	We'll send a mechanic.
Wie ist …	*vee ist*	What is your …
Ihr Autokennzeichen?	*eer **ow**tokenntsiyken*	car registration?
Ihre Ausweisnummer?	*eere **ows**viysnoommer*	passport number?
Ihre Versicherungs-nummer?	*fer**zi**sheroongsnoom-mer*	insurance number?
Ihre Papiere, bitte.	*eere pa**pee**re **bit**te*	Show me your papers, please.
Kommen Sie später wieder.	*kommen zee **shpay**ter **vee**der*	Come back later.

main car parts

accelerator	das Gaspedal	*das **gaas**pedaal*
battery	die Batterie	*dee batte**ree***
brakes	die Bremsen	*dee **brem**zen*
clutch	die Kupplung	*dee **koopp**loong*
engine	der Motor	*der **moh**tor*
radiator	der Kühler	*der **kew**ler*
steering wheel	das Steuerrad	*das **shtoy**erraat*
tools	das Werkzeug	*das **vayrk**tsoyg*
tyres	die Reifen	*dee **riy**fen*
wheels	die Räder	*dee **ray**der*
windows	die Scheiben	*dee **shiy**ben*
windscreen	die Windschutzscheibe	*dee **vint**shootsshiybe*
wiper	der Scheibenwischer	*der **shiy**benvisher*

check out 4

Your car has broken down, so you call a mechanic from an emergency phone.

- ○ Ich habe eine Panne. Könnten Sie mir bitte helfen?
  *ish **haa**be **iy**ne panne. **kern**nten zee meer **bit**te **hel**fen*

- Wo sind Sie?
  voh zint zee

- ○ Ich bin auf der A25, fünfzig Kilometer vor Hamburg.
  *ish bin owf der aa fewnfoont**tsvan**tsig **fewnf**tseeg keelo**may**ter fohr **ham**boork*

- Was ist das Problem?
  *vas ist das pro**blaym***

- ○ Die Bremsen funktionieren nicht.
  *dee **brem**zen foonktsyoh**nee**ren nisht*

- Wir schicken jemanden in einer halben Stunde.
  *veer **shi**ken **yay**manden in **iy**ner **hal**ben **shtoon**de*

Q What's wrong with your car?
Someone will come straight away: true or false?

128

sound check

In German the sounds **au** and **eu** are pronounced differently than in English.

au is similar to the English sound 'ow' in 'cow':

Krankenhaus *kran*kenhows   ausfüllen *ows*fewllen

eu is pronounced like 'oy' as in 'boy':

Werkzeug *vayrk*tsoyk   heute *hoy*te

try it out

doctor's orders

Read the labels below and work out what you should or shouldn't do.

1   Einmal täglich morgens nehmen.
2   Kauen, nicht schlucken.
3   Nach dem Essen nehmen.
4   Kontakt mit Augen vermeiden.

as if you were there

You're suffering from a sore throat and go to the chemist's. Follow the prompts to play your part.

Guten Tag. Was kann ich für Sie tun?

(Say your throat hurts)
Haben Sie eine Erkältung?

(Say yes, and ask if he can recommend something)
Nehmen Sie diese Tabletten mit Wasser.

(Ask how many times a day you should take them)
Zweimal täglich.

linkup

saying what's yours

German is similar to English when you're saying who something belongs to:

Ich habe **meinen** Koffer verloren. I have lost **my** suitcase.
Unser Flugzeug fliegt um elf Uhr. **Our** plane leaves at 11 o'clock.

saying what hurts

There are two main ways of expressing pain. You can use wehtun, which splits in two separate words when it's used in a sentence:

Mein Kopf tut weh. My head hurts. (to say one thing hurts)
Meine Füße tun weh. My feet hurt. (to say more than one thing hurts)

Or you can add -schmerzen (ache or pain) to a part of the body:
Ich habe Kopfschmerzen. I have a headache.

Language **Builder**

Using the words and phrases in this book will enable you to deal with most everyday situations. If you want to go a bit further and start building your own phrases, there are a few rules about German that will help you.

ways of saying 'you'

There are three different ways of saying 'you' in German. Use Sie to one or more persons in more formal situations and to be polite (to shopkeepers, waiters, etc.) and du to one person who you're on familiar terms with. Use ihr to more than one person who you're on familiar terms with. If in doubt, use Sie.

Here are three ways of asking 'When are you coming?'
Wann kommen Sie? (to one or more persons)
Wann kommst du? (to one person who you know well)
Wann kommt ihr? (to two or more people who you know well)

gender

German nouns (words for people, things, places, etc.) are either masculine, feminine or neuter. They always start with a capital letter:

masculine nouns	feminine nouns	neuter nouns
der Zug the train	die Kathedrale the cathedral	das Auto the car
der Bus the bus	die Straße the street	das Zimmer the room

articles ('the' & 'a')

In German there are different ways of saying 'the' depending on whether the noun is masculine, feminine, neuter or plural. These forms change according to the noun's function in the sentence.

The nominative (dictionary form) shows the subject of the sentence:

Der Bus kommt. The bus is coming.
Die Kathedrale ist schön. The cathedral is beautiful.
Das Eis kostet einen Euro. The ice cream costs €1.

The accusative shows the object (i.e. what you want, have, or are looking for):

Ich nehme **den Bus.** I'm taking the bus.
Ich suche **die Kathedrale.** I'm looking for the cathedral.
Ich möchte **das Eis.** I'd like the ice cream.
It is also used after some prepositions, such as für, ohne, um:
Das Glas ist **für den Wein.** The glass is for the wine.

The dative is used after many prepositions, e.g. mit, nach, von:

Ich komme **mit dem Fahrrad.** I'm coming by bicycle.

the	masculine	feminine	neuter	plural
nominative	der	die	das	die
accusative	den	die	das	die
dative	dem	der	dem	den

a	masculine	feminine	neuter
nominative	ein	eine	ein
accusative	einen	eine	ein
dative	einem	einer	einem

There are also both masculine and feminine forms of occupations. The feminine form mostly ends in **-in**. For example:

der Manager/die Managerin manager
der Student/die Studentin student
der Zahnarzt/die Zahnärztin dentist

Language **Builder**

plurals

There is no set rule for forming plurals in German. The best way to remember them is to learn the plural form every time you meet a new word.

Most feminine nouns add **-n** or **-en** to form the plural (die Woche/die Wochen; die Packung, die Packungen). The other main patterns you'll see are:

add	singular	plural
-e	der Tag	die Tage
-¨-	der Bruder	die Brüder
¨-e	der Bahnhof	die Bahnhöfe
-er	das Kind	die Kinder
¨-er	das Land	die Länder
	das Zimmer	die Zimmer
-s	das Foto	die Fotos

verbs & pronouns

Verb endings change according to the person doing the action. Here is an example:

Ich kauf**e** die Briefmarken. I buy/I am buying the stamps.
Du kauf**st** die Briefmarken. You buy/You are buying the stamps.

When you look up a word in the dictionary, you will find it in its basic form, 'the infinitive'. Almost all German infinitives end in **-en**. To form regular verbs, remove the **-en**, then add the endings below.

kaufen – to buy			
ich kauf**e**	I buy	wir kauf**en**	we buy
du kauf**st**	you buy	ihr kauf**t**	you buy
er/sie/es kauf**t**	he/she/it buys	sie kauf**en**	they buy

There are some verbs that follow this pattern except for the du and the er/sie/es forms, where they add an Umlaut (¨):
fahren to go/drive
Ich **fahre** nach Berlin. I'm going to Berlin.
but Sie **fährt** nach Bonn. She's going to Bonn.

There are also irregular verbs, which don't follow a pattern and have to be learned. Two very useful irregular verbs are haben (to have) and sein (to be).

ich habe – I have	
du hast	you have
er/sie hat	he/she has
wir haben	we have
ihr habt	you have
Sie haben	you have

ich bin – I am	
du bist	you are
er/sie ist	he/she is
wir sind	we are
ihr seid	you are
Sie sind	you are

possessives ('my'/'your')

In order to identify whose something is, you might need:
Mein Name ist Clarke. My name is Clarke.
Wie ist **dein/Ihr** Name? What's your name? (informal/formal)
Unser Hotel ist gut. Our hotel is good.

Possessives change according to the number and gender of the noun they refer to, e.g. mein Buch (neuter) my book but mein**e** Bank (feminine) my bank and mein**e** Schuhe (plural) my shoes. They also change according to case, e.g. Ich suche mein**en** Hut. I'm looking for my hat. For these changes, they take the same forms as ein (see p132).

Language **Builder**

question words

It is always very helpful to know how to ask about things. As in English, you put the question word(s) at the beginning of a sentence:

Was ist das? What is this?
Wie viele sind da? How many are there?
Wie viel kostet das? How much is that?
Wo ist das? Where is that?
Wie komme ich zum Bahnhof? How do I get to the station?
Wann fährt der Bus? When does the bus leave?
Wohin fährt er? Where does it go to?
Woher kommen Sie? Where do you come from?
Wer ist das? Who is that?

word order

If you stick to short sentences, the word order is fairly easy. The structure of a simple sentence is the same as in English:

subject	verb	object
Ich	kaufe	eine CD.
I	buy	a CD.
Er	trinkt	ein Bier.
He	drinks	a beer.

When there are two verbs in a sentence, you put the second one at the end. This verb stays in the infinitive or '-en' form:
Ich gehe schwimmen. I'm going swimming.

The sentence structure only becomes noticeably different from English, when more information is included:
Ich möchte eine CD **kaufen**. I want to buy a CD.
Können Sie mir **helfen**? Can you help me?
Könnte ich das Zimmer **sehen**? Could I see the room?

prepositions

Words such as 'in', 'on' and 'for' are called prepositions. They are normally followed by a noun and are often used to specify where things are located. The main prepositions in German are:

an	at	ohne	without
auf	on	über	above
durch	through	um	around
für	for	unter	under
hinter	behind	vor	in front of
in	in	von	from
mit	with	zu	to
nach	to	zwischen	between
neben	next to		

Many prepositions are followed by the dative:
mit **dem** Rad   by bicycle
but some are followed by the accusative:
Wir fahren um **den** Bahnhof.   We're driving around the station.

Certain prepositions combine with the masculine and neuter word for 'the':
in   + dem → im
von + dem → vom
an   + dem → am
zu   + dem → zum

Certain combinations are so common that they quickly become second nature:
mit dem Bus   by bus
am Freitag   on Friday
zum Bahnhof   to the station

Language **Builder**

adjectives

Adjectives (describing words) are used to provide more information about nouns. When they stand on their own at the end of a sentence, they are used the same way as in English:

Das Hotel ist teuer.   The hotel is expensive.

Das Essen schmeckt fantastisch.   The food tastes fantastic.

comparatives

As the name suggests, comparatives are used for making comparisons. To produce the comparative form, it's usually safe just to add -er to the adjective:

Mein Zimmer ist schön.   My room is nice.

Dein Zimmer ist schön**er**.   Your room is nicer.

Berlin ist weit.   Berlin is far.

Dresden ist weit**er**.   Dresden is further.

In order to say that something is too small, or too expensive, all you have to do is to put 'zu' in front of the adjective:

Das Auto ist zu klein.   The car is too small.

Das Zimmer ist zu teuer.   The room is too expensive.

As always, there are a few exceptions to the rules. Here are the most common and useful ones:

gut → besser   good → better
viel → mehr   a lot → more
teuer → teurer   expensive → more expensive
hoch → höher   high → higher
lang → länger   long → longer
kurz → kürzer   short → shorter

Bare Necessities......

check out

1 the station; straight on
2 You ask whether he speaks English.
3 on business; it's very interesting

lucky numbers

a Ruth Städing
b Peter Wiese
c Claudia Hauswirt

as if you were there

Guten Abend. Gut, danke.

goohten aabent. gooht danke

Ich heiße Sarah.

ish hiysse sayra

Ich bin Engländerin. Ich komme aus Manchester.

ish bin englenderin. ish komme ows mentshester

Getting Around........

check out

1 the next street on the left; about 500m
2 your driver's licence; for one week
3 the first street; about 100km
4 leaves 8.17; arrives 10.03; from platform 14
5 false, you're asked if you want 1st or 2nd class; €200

mind the gap

1 zurück; Platz; Gleis
2 Wo; Straße

as if you were there

Entschuldigung, wo ist die Touristeninformation, bitte?

entshooldigoong voh ist dee tooristeninformatsyohn bitte

Ist das weit von hier?

ist das viyt fon heer

Gibt es hier in der Nähe eine Bank?

geept es heer in der naye iyne bank

Somewhere to Stay....

check out

1 for one week; €343
2 by 10am; from 7 to 9am
3 a caravan; two adults and two children

in the mix

1 Einzelzimmer
2 Dusche
3 Zimmerschlüssel
4 Kinderbett
5 Fernseher
6 Klimaanlage

match it up

1e; 2d; 3b; 4a; 5c

as if you were there

Ich möchte ein Doppelzimmer und ein Einzelzimmer.

ish mershte iyn doppeltsimmer oont iyn iyntseltsimmer

Für vier Nächte, bitte. Hat das Doppelzimmer ein Telefon?

*fewr feer **nesh**te **bi**tte. hat das **dopp**leltsimmer iyn **te**lefohn*

Mit Dusche, bitte.

*mit **doo**she **bi**tte*

Buying Things..........

check out

1 false; €10.80
2 He asks what size you are; The trousers are the most expensive (€59) and the gloves the cheapest (€20).
3 55 cents; a €10 phone card

money talk

Total: €5,35

as if you were there

Wie viel kosten die Kirschen?

*vee feel **kos**ten dee **kir**shen*

Zwei Kilo, bitte.

*tsviy **kee**lo **bi**tte*

Haben Sie Erdbeeren?

***haa**ben zee **ayrt**bayren*

Dreihundert Gramm.

***driy**hoondert gramm*

Danke, das ist alles.

***dan**ke das ist **a**lles*

Café Life.................

check out

1 apple cake; a cup of hot chocolate
2 false, Black Forest gateau

question time

1b 2a 3b 4c

in the mix

f, c, b, e, g, a, d

as if you were there

Ich möchte ein Stück Apfelkuchen.

*ish **mersh**te iyn shtewk **ap**felkoohken*

Haben Sie Schokoladentorte?

***haa**ben zee shoko**laa**dentorte*

Eine Tasse Kaffee, bitte.

*iyne **ta**sse **ka**ffay **bi**tte*

Eating Out...............

check out

1 three people; ten minutes
2 today's special; chicken
3 glass or a bottle of wine
4 Did you like the food? Do you want anything else?

match it up

1d 2f 3c 4e 5b 6a

as if you were there

Die Speisekarte, bitte.

*dee **shpiy**zekarte **bi**tte*

Ich möchte bestellen.

*ish **mersh**te be**shte**llen*

Können Sie etwas empfehlen?

*ker*nnen zee *et*vas em*pfay*len

Danke. Ich möchte ein Kotelett mit Kartoffeln und einen Salat.

*dan*ke ish *mersh*te iyn kot*lett* mit kar*to*ffeln oont *iy*nen za*laat*

Ja, das Essen war gut. Ich möchte zahlen, bitte.

*yaa das *e*ssen vaar gooht ish *mersh*te tsaa*len *bi*tte*

Entertainment..........

check out

1 by the station, in Ottostrasse; 9am-4pm
2 €62; 4 hours
3 €2.60; false, you ask where the changing rooms are
4 windsurfing; no, it's too dangerous

all mixed up

1 Ausstellung
2 Kino
3 Theater
4 Nachtclub
5 Schwimmbad
6 Tennisspiel

as if you were there

Wo fährt der Bus ab?

voh fayrt der boos ap

Wie lange dauert die Fahrt?

*vee *lan*ge *dow*ert dee faart*

Wo bekomme ich die Karten, bitte?

*voh be*ko*mme ish dee *kar*ten *bi*tte*

Emergencies............

check out

1 a large or a small packet (of tablets)
2 false: he asks what you have eaten; yes, he will
3 your money; the Hotel zur Post
4 the brakes aren't working; false: in half an hour

doctor's orders

1 Take once a day in the morning.
2 Chew, don't swallow whole.
3 Take after meals.
4 Avoid contact with eyes.

as if you were there

Mein Hals tut weh.

miyn hals tooht vay

Ja. Können Sie etwas empfehlen?

*yaa. *ker*nnen zee *et*vas em*pfay*len*

A

about ungefähr *oongefayr*
accelerator Gaspedal, das *gaaspedaal*
accident Unfall, der *oohnfall*
address Adresse, die *adresse*
admission Eintritt, der *iyntritt*
adult Erwachsene(r), der/die *ervaksene(r)*
aeroplane Flugzeug, das *floohktsoyk*
after nach *naak*
afternoon Nachmittag, der *nakmittaak*
 in the afternoon nachmittags *nakmittaaks*
again wieder *veeder*
against gegen *gaygen*
air Luft, die *looft*
air-conditioning Klimaanlage, die *kleema-anlaage*
airmail Luftpost, die *looftpost*
airport Flughafen, der *floohkhaafen*
alarm clock Wecker, der *veker*
alcohol Alkohol, der *alkohohl*
alcoholic alkoholisch *alkohohlish*
allergic allergisch *allayrgish*
allergy Allergie, die *allergee*
to be allowed dürfen *dewrfen*
also auch *owk*
ambulance Krankenwagen, der *krankenvaagen*
and und *oont*
angora Angorawolle, die *angohravolle*
ankle Fußknöchel, der *foohssknewshel*
anything else? sonst noch etwas? *zonst nok etvas*
apart from außer *owsser*
apple Apfel, der *apfel*
approach road Auffahrt, die *owffaart*
arm Arm, der *aarm*
arrival Ankunft, die *ankoonft*
art Kunst, die *koonst*
as far as bis *bis*
ash tray Aschenbecher, der *ashenbesher*
at an *an*
to attack (mug) überfallen *ewberfallen*

B

back Rücken, der *rewken*
backache Rückenschmerzen, die (pl) *rewkenshmertsen*
bad schlimm *shlimm*
bag Tasche, die *tashe*
bakery Bäckerei, die *bekeriy*
balcony Balkon, der *balkohn*
ball Ball, der *ball*

ball-point pen Kugelschreiber, der *koohgelshriyber*
banana Banane, die *banaane*
bank Bank, die *bank*
bar Bar, die *baar*
basement Untergeschoss, das *oontergeshoss*
basket Korb, der *kohrp*
bath Bad, das *baat*
bathroom Badezimmer, das *baadetsimmer*
battery Batterie, die *batteree*
to be sein *ziyn*
beach Strand, der *shtrant*
beach towel Badetuch, das *baadetoohk*
beautiful schön *shern*
beaker Becher, der *besher*
to become werden *vayrden*
bed Bett, das *bett*
beer Bier, das *beer*
beer garden Biergarten, der *beergarten*
before vor *fohr*
to begin beginnen, anfangen *beginnen, anfangen*
beginning Beginn, der, Anfang, der *beginn, anfang*
behind hinter *hinter*
to believe glauben *glowben*
belt Gürtel, der *gewrtel, der*
better besser *besser*
bicycle Fahrrad, das *faarraat, das*
big groß *grohss*
bikini Bikini, der *bikeenee*
bill Rechnung, die *reshnoong*
a bit ein bisschen *iyn bissshen*
to bite beißen, stechen *biyssen, shteshen*
black schwarz *shvarts*
blind Rollo, das *rollo*
blouse Bluse, die *bloohze*
blue blau *blow*
boarding house Pension, die *pangzyohn*
boat Boot, das *boht*
bone Knochen, der *knoken*
book Buch, das *boohk*
book shop Buchhandlung, die *boohkhandloong*
boot Stiefel, der *shteefel*
bottle Flasche, die *flashe*
brake Bremse, die *bremze*
bread Brot, das *broht*
bread roll Brötchen, das *brertshen*
break Pause, die *powze,*
to break down eine Panne haben *iyne panne haaben*

breakfast Frühstück, das *frewshtewk*
bridge Brücke, die *brewke*
briefcase Aktenkoffer, der *aktenkoffer*
broken gebrochen *gebroken*
brown braun *brown*
burn Verbrennung, die *ferbrennoong*
burnt verbrannt *ferbrannt*
bus Bus, der *boos*
bus stop Bushaltestelle, die *booshalteshtelle*
bus tour Busrundfahrt, die *boosroontfaart*
business Geschäft, das *gesheft*
business man/woman Geschäftsmann/frau, der/die *geshefts*mann/*frow*
business trip Geschäftsreise, die *geshefts*ryz
but aber *aaber*
butcher Fleischer, der, Metzger, der *fliysher metsger*
butter Butter, die *bootter*
to buy kaufen *kowfen*
bye tschüss *tshewss*

C

cabbage Weißkohl, der *viysskohl*
café Café, das *kafey*
cake Kuchen, der *koohken*
to call anrufen *anroohfen*
to be called heißen *hiyssen*
camping site Campingplatz, der *kempingplats*
can Dose, die *dohze*
car Auto, das *owto*
car park Parkplatz, der *paarkplats*
car wash Waschstraße, die *vashshtraasse*
carafe Karaffe, die *karaffe*
caravan Wohnwagen, der *vohnvaagen*
cash bar *baar*
cash machine Geldautomat, der *geltowtomaat*
cassette Kassette, die *kassette*
castle Schloss, das *shloss*
casualty department Unfallstation, die *oohnfallshtatsyohn*
cat Katze, die *katse*
catalogue Katalog, der *katalohg*
to catch (bus, train) nehmen *naymen*
cathedral Kathedrale, die *katedraale*
CD CD, die *tsayday*
centre Zentrum, das *tsentroom*
chain Kette, die *kette*
chair Stuhl, der *shtoohl*
champagne Champagner, der *shampanyer*
change Wechselgeld, das *vekselgelt*

change (loose money) Kleingeld, das *kliyngelt*
to change tauschen *towshen*
to change (trains) umsteigen *oomshtiygen*
changing room Umkleidekabine, die *oomkliydekabeene*
charge Gebühr, die *gebewr*
cheap billig *billig*
to check out (hotel room) verlassen *ferlassen*
cheese Käse, der *kayze*
chemist's (pharmacy) Apotheke, die *apotayke*
cherry Kirsche, die *kirshe*
chest Brust, die *broost*
child Kind, das *kint*
children's bed Kinderbett, das *kinderbett*
chin Kinn, das *kinn*
chips Pommes frites, die (pl) *pomm frits*
chocolate Schokolade, die *shokolaade*
chocolate cake Schokoladenkuchen, der *shokolaadenkoohken*
chocolate gâteau Schokoladentorte, die *shokolaadentorte*
to choose wählen *vaylen*
church Kirche, die *keershe*
cigarette Zigarette, die *tsigarette*
cinema Kino, das *keeno*
city Stadt, die *shtat*
city centre Innenstadt, die *innenshtat*
climb steigen *shtiygen*
cloakroom Garderobe, die *garderohbe*
clock Uhr, die *oohr*
clothes' shop Bekleidungsgeschäft, das *bekliydoongsgesheft*
clutch Kupplung, die *kooploong*
coat Mantel, der *mantel*
coffee Kaffee, der *kaffay*
cola Cola, die/das *kohla*
cold kalt *kalt*
to have a cold eine Erkältung haben *erkeltoong*
colour Farbe, die *faarbe*
to come kommen *kommen*
commission Kommission, die *kommissyohn*
concert Konzert, das *kontsert*
concession Ermäßigung, die *ermayssigoong*
conference room Konferenzraum, der *konferentsrowm*
to contain enthalten *enthalten*
to continue weitergehen *viytergayen*
to be convenient passen *passen*
corner Ecke, die *eke*

correct richtig *rishtig*
to cost kosten *kosten*
cotton Baumwolle, die *bowmvolle*
couchette Schlafwagen, der *shlaafvaagen*
couchette (berth) Platz im Schlafwagen, der *plats im shlaafvaagen*
cough Husten, der *hoohsten*
to cough husten *hoohsten*
cough medicine Hustensaft, der *hoohstenzaft*
to count zählen *tsaylen*
counter Schalter, der *shalter*
of course natürlich, selbstverständlich *natewrlish, zelpstfershtendlish*
court (law) Gericht, das *gerisht*
court (tennis) Platz, der *plats*
cowbell Kuhglocke, die *koohgloke*
cream (cosmetics) Creme, die *krem*
cream (food) Sahne, die *zaane*
credit card Kreditkarte, die *kredeetkarte*
cross-country run Geländelauf, der *gelendelowf*
crossing Kreuzung, die *kroytsoong*
cuckoo clock Kuckucksuhr, die *kookooksoohr*
cucumber Gurke, die *goorke*
cul-de-sac Sackgasse, die *zakgasse*
cultural kulturell *kooltoorell*
culture Kultur, die *kooltoohr*
cup Tasse, die *tasse*
cupboard Schrank, der *shrank*
to cut schneiden *shniyden*
cutlery Besteck, das *beshtek*
to cycle Fahrrad fahren *faarrat faaren*
cycle path Fahrradweg, der *faarratwayg*

D

daily täglich *tayglish*
daily travel card Tageskarte, die *taageskarte*
dark bread Schwarzbrot, das *shvartsbroht*
day Tag, der *taak*
decaffeinated coffee koffeinfreier Kaffee, der *koffayeenfriyer kaffay*
deckchair Liegestuhl, der *leegeshtoohl*
to depart (train, bus) abfahren *apfaaren*
department store Kaufhaus, das *kowfhows*
dessert Nachtisch, der *naaktish*
dessert bowl Schale, die *shaale*
to develop entwickeln *entvikeln*
to dial wählen *vaylen*

difficult schwierig *shveerig*
digital camera Digitalkamera, die *digitaalkamera*
dining-room Speisesaal, der *shpiyzezaal*
dish Gericht, das *gerisht*
dish of the day Tagesgericht, das *taagesgerisht*
disposable camera Wegwerfkamera, die *vekvayrfkamera*
diversion Umleitung, die *oomliytoong,*
to do tun, machen *toohn, maken*
doctor Arzt, der/Ärztin, die *aartst, der/ayrtstin*
dog Hund, der *hoont*
doll Puppe, die *poope*
double room Doppelzimmer, das *doppeltsimmer*
downhill skiing Abfahrtslauf, der *apfaartslowf*
downstairs unten *oonten*
dress Kleid, das *kliyt*
drink Getränk, das *getrenk*
to drink trinken *trinken*
to drive fahren *faaren*
driver Fahrer, der *faarer*
driving licence Führerschein, der *fewrershiyn*
drop Tropfen, der *tropfen*

E

ear Ohr, das *ohr,*
easy einfach *iynfak*
to eat essen *essen*
egg Ei, das *iy*
elbow Ellbogen, der *ellbohgen*
emergency exit Notausgang, der *nohtowsgang*
end Ende, das *ende*
engine Motor, der *mohtor*
entertainment guide Veranstaltungskalender, der *feranshtaltoongskalender*
entrance Eingang, der *iyngang*
espresso Espresso, der *espresso*
European Health Insurance Card, EHIC Europäische Krankenversicherungskarte *oyropayishe krankenferzisheroongskarte*
evening Abend, der *aabent*
in the evening abends *aabents*
evening meal Abendessen, das *aabentessen*
everyone alle *alle*
everything alles *alles*

everything okay? alles in Ordnung?
*alles in ort*noong

to examine untersuchen *oonterzoohken*
excellent ausgezeichnet *owsgetsiyshnet*
to exchange (money) wechseln *vekseln*
exchange rate Kurs, der *koors*
Excuse me! Entschuldigung!
entshooldigoong
exhibition Ausstellung, die
owsshtelloong
exit Ausgang, der *owsgang*
exit (motorway) Abfahrt, die *apfaart*
expensive teuer *toyer*

F

eye Auge, das *owge*
fair Messe, die *messe*
fairly ziemlich *tseemlish*
family Familie, die *fameelye*
fantastic fantastisch *fantastish*
far weit *viyt*
to feel fühlen *fewlen*
fever Fieber, das *feeber*
to fill out ausfüllen *owsfewllen*
to fill up (with petrol) voll tanken
folltanken
filling Plombe, die *plombe*
film Film, der *film*
to find finden *finden*
finger Finger, der *finger*
finished (over) zu Ende *tsooh ende*
finished (ready) fertig *fertig*
fire brigade Feuerwehr, die *foyervayr*
fireworks Feuerwerk, das *foyervayrk*
first erste *erste*
first-aid box Verbandskasten, der
ferbantskasten
fish Fisch, der *fish*
flea market Flohmarkt, der *flohmarkt*
floor Stock, der, Etage, die *shtok,*
etaashe
flounder Flunder, die *floonder*
fondue Fondue, das *fondew*
food Essen, das *essen*
foot Fuß, der *foohss*
football Fußball, der *foohssball*
football match Fußballspiel, das
foohssballshpeel
fork Gabel, die *gaabe*
form Formular, das *formulaar*
free frei *friy*
fried gebraten *gebraaten*
from von *fon*
in front of vor *fohr*
fruit Obst, das *ohpst*
fruit flan Obstkuchen, der
ohpstkoohken
full board Vollpension, die
follpangzyohn

G

gallery Galerie, die *galeree*
game Spiel, das *shpeel*
garage (parking) Garage *garaashe*
garage (petrol) Tankstelle, die
tankshtelle
garage (repairs) Autowerkstatt, die
owtovayrkshtatt
garden Garten, der *garten*
gâteau Torte, die *torte*
to get (receive) bekommen *bekommen*
to get (fetch) holen *hohlen*
to get off (train, bus) aussteigen
owsshtiygen
to get up aufstehen *owfshtayen*
gingerbread Lebkuchen, der
laypkoohken
to give geben *gayben*
glass Glas, das *glaas*
glasses Brille, die *brille*
glossy (photos) Hochglanz, der
hohkglants
glove Handschuh, der *hantshooh*
to go gehen, (by train, bus) fahren
gayen, faaren
golf Golf, das *golf*
golf club Golfschläger, der *golfshlayger*
golf course Golfplatz, der *golfplats*
good gut *gooht*
goodbye Auf Wiedersehen *owf*
veederzayen
gramme Gramm, das *gramm*
grape Traube, die *trowbe*
grape juice Traubensaft, der
trowbenzaft
green grün *grewn*
grilled gegrillt *gegrillt*
ground floor Erdgeschoss, das
ayrtgeshoss
to grow wachsen *vaksen*
guesthouse Pension, die *pangzyohn*
guestroom Gästezimmer, das
gestetsimmer
guided tour Führung, die *fewroong*
gym Fitnessraum, der *fitnessrowm*

H

hair Haar, das *haar*
hairdryer Haartrockner, der *haartrokner*
half Hälfte, die, halb *helfte halp*
half-board Halbpension, die
halppangzyohn
ham Schinken, der *shinken*
hand Hand, die *hant*
to hand in abgeben *apgayben*
handbag Handtasche, die *hanttashe*
to happen passieren *passeeren*
happy froh, glücklich *froh, glewklish*

hat Hut, der *hooht*
to have haben *haaben*
to have to müssen *mewssen*
hayfever Heuschnupfen der
  hoyshnoopfen
he er *ayr*
head Kopf, der *kopf*
headache Kopfschmerzen, die (pl)
  kopfshmertsen
headache tablet Kopfschmerztablette,
  die *kopfshmertstablette*
heart Herz, das *herts*
heart attack Herzanfall, der,
  Herzinfarkt, der *hertsanfall,*
  hertsinfarkt
heating Heizung, die *hiytsoong*
hello hallo *hallo*
help Hilfe, die *hilfe*
to help helfen *helfen*
her sie, ihr *zee, eer*
here hier *heer*
high hoch *hohk*
high chair Babystuhl, der
  baybeeshtoohl
to go hiking wandern *vandern*
hill Hügel, der Berg, der *hewgel*
  bayrk
hip Hüfte, die *hewfte*
to hire mieten, liehen *meeten, liyen*
to hold halten *halten*
holiday Urlaub, der *oohrlowp*
holidays Ferien, die (pl) *fayryen*
home-made hausgemacht
  howsgemakt
hospital Krankenhaus, das
  krankenhows
hot heiß *hiyss*
hotel Hotel, das *hotel*
hour Stunde, die *shtoonde*
house Haus, das *hows*
household goods department
  Haushaltsabteilung, die
  howshaltsaptiyloong
how wie *vee*
to hurt weh tun *vay toohn*
hurt verletzt *ferletst*
it hurts es tut weh *es tooht vay*

I

I ich *ish*
ice cream Eis, das *iys*
ice cream parlour Eisdiele, die
  iysdeele
ID papers Papiere, die (pl) *papeere*
identity card Ausweis, der *owsviys*
immediately gleich, sofort *gliysh,*
  zofort

in in *in*
inclusive inklusive *inkloozeeve*
indigestion Verdauungsbeschwerden,
  die *ferdowoongsbeshvayrde*
infection Infektion, die *infektsyohn*
information Auskunft, die
  Information, die *owskoonft*
  informatsyohn
injured verletzt *ferletst*
inline skates Inline-Skates, die
  inliynskayts
insurance Versicherung, die
  ferzisheroong
insurance number
  Versicherungsnummer, die
  ferzisheroongsnoommer
to be interested in sich interessieren
  für *zish interesseeren fewr*
  I'm interested in ich interessiere
  mich für *ish interesseere mish fewr*
interesting interessant *interessant*
international international
  internatsyonaal
internet access Internetzugang, der
  internettsoohgang
internet café Internetcafé, das
  internetkaffay
interval Pause, die *powze*
to introduce vorstellen *fohrshtellen*
iron Bügeleisen, das *bewgeliyzen*
to iron bügeln *bewgeln*
it es *es*

J

jacket Jacke, die *yake*
jacket (of suit) Jackett, das *dshakett*
jeans Jeans, die (pl) *dsheens*
jewellery Schmuck, der *shmook*
job Beruf, der *beroohf*
journey Fahrt, die, Reise, die *faart*
  riyze
jug Krug, der *kroohk*
juice Saft, der *zaft*
jeweller's Schmuckgeschäft, das,
  Juwelier, der *shmookgesheft*
  yooveleer

K

ketchup Ketchup, der/das *ketshap*
key Schlüssel, der *shlewssel*
kidney Niere, die *neere*
kilo Kilo, das *keeloh*
kilometre Kilometer, der
  keelohmayter
kiosk Kiosk, der *keeosk*
kiwi fruit Kiwi, die *keevee*
knee Knie, das *knee*
knife Messer, das *messer*
to know wissen *vissen*

L

ladies' fashion department
  Damenabteilung, die
  daamenaptiyloong
lady Dame, die *daame*
lake See, der *zay*
laptop Laptop, der *leptop*
late spät *shpayt*
launderette Waschsalon, der
  vashzalong
leather Leder, das *layder*
to leave verlassen *ferlassen*
left links *links*
leg Bein, das *biyn*
lemon Zitrone, die *tsitrohne*
lemonade Limonade, die *limonaade*
lesson Unterricht, der *oonterrisht*
to let vermieten *fermeeten*
letter Brief, der *breef*
to lie liegen *leegen*
to lie down sich hinlegen *zish hinlaygen*
lift Fahrstuhl, der *faarshtoohl*
light Licht, das *lisht*
light bulb Glühbirne, die *glewbirne*
lighter (for cigarettes) Feuerzeug, das
  foyertsoyk
to like mögen *mergen*
  I like it ich mag es, es gefällt mir *ish
  maak es es gefellt meer*
litre Liter, der *leeter*
little wenig *vaynig*
a little ein bisschen, ein wenig *iyn
  bissshen iyn vaynig*
to live wohnen *vohnen*
liver Leber, die *layber*
lock Schloss, das *shloss*
locker Schrank, der *shrank*
lycra Lycra, das *liykra*
to look schauen *showen*
to look for suchen *zoohken*
I'm looking forward to ich freue mich
  auf *ish froye mish owf*
to look like aussehen *owszayen*
long lang *lang*
to lose verlieren *ferleeren*
lost property office Fundbüro, das
  foontbewro
a lot viel *feel*
low niedrig *needrig*
luck Glück, das *glewk*
luggage Gepäck, das *gepek*
lunch Mittagessen, das *mittaakessen*
lunch time mittags *mittaaks*

M

magazine Zeitschrift, die *tsyitshrift*
main course Hauptgericht, das,
  Hauptspeise, die *howptgerisht
  howptshpiyze*
main station Hauptbahnhof, der
  howptbaanhohf
to make tun, machen *toohn, maken*
man Mann, der *mann*
map Stadtplan, der *shtatplaan*
margarine Margarine, die *margareene*
market Markt, der *markt*
market place Marktplatz, der
  marktplats
match Spiel, das *shpeel*
matt matt *matt*
may dürfen *dewrfen*
to mean bedeuten *bedoyten*
meat Fleisch, das *fliysh*
medicine Medikament, das, Medizin, die
  medikament meditseen
melon Melone, die *melohne*
membership card Mitgliedsausweis, der
  mitgleedsowsviys
memory card Speicherkarte, die
  shpiysherkarte
men's fashion department
  Herrenabteilung, die *herrenaptiyloong*
menu Speisekarte, die *shpiyzekarte,*
milk Milch, die *milsh*
mineral water Mineralwasser, das
  mineraalvasser
mirror Spiegel, der *shpeegel*
mistake Fehler, der *fayler*
mixed gemischt *gemisht*
mobile phone Handy, das *hendee*
moment Moment, der *moment*
money Geld, das *gelt*
more mehr *mayr*
morning Morgen, der *morgen*
in the morning morgens *morgens*
motorway Autobahn, die *owtobaan*
mountain Berg, der *bayrk*
mountain bike Mountainbike, das
  mowntenbiyk
to go mountain-biking Mountainbike
  fahren *mowntenbiyk faaren*
mountaineering Bergsteigen, das
  bayrkshtiygen
mouth Mund, der *moont*
mp3 player MP3-Player, der *empaydriy-
  player*
Mr Herr *herr*
Mrs Frau *frow*
much viel *feel*
to mug überfallen *ewberfallen*
museum Museum, das *moozayoom*
musical Musical, das *mewzikl*
mussel Muschel, die *mooshel*
must müssen *mewssen*
mustard Senf, der *zenf*

N

nail Nagel, der *naagel*
name Name, der *naame*
napkin Serviette, die *zervyette*
nausea Übelkeit, die *ewbelkiyt*
near nah *naa*
nearby in der Nähe *in der naye*
neck Genick, das *genick*
to need brauchen *browken*
new neu *noy*
newsagent's Zeitschriftenhändler, der *tsiytshriftenhendler*
newspaper Zeitung, die *tsiytoong*
next nächste *naykste*
next to neben *nayben*
night nacht, die *nakt*
  at night nachts *nakts*
nightclub Nachtklub, der *naktkloop*
no nein *niyn*
no one niemand *neemant*
non-alcoholic alkoholfrei *alkohohlfriy*
non-smoker Nichtraucher, der *nishtrowker*
not nicht *nisht*
notepaper Briefpapier, das *breefpapeer*
nothing nichts *nishts*
nought null *nooll*
number Nummer, die *noommer*
numbered nummeriert *noommereert*
nylon Nylon, das *niylon*

O

occupation Beruf, der *beroohf*
often oft *oft*
oil Öl, das *erl*
old town Altstadt, die *altshtat*
on auf *owf*
once einmal *iynmaal*
one way street Einbahnstraße, die *iynbaanshtraasse*
onion tart Zwiebelkuchen, der *tsveebelkoohken*
only nur *noohr*
opening hours Öffnungszeiten, die (pl) *erffnoongstsiyten*
opera Oper, die *ohper*
to operate operieren *opereeren*
opposite gegenüber *gaygenewber*
optician's Optiker, der *optiker*
orange orange *orangsh*
orange juice Orangensaft, der *orangshenzaft*
to order bestellen *beshtellen*
out of order außer Betrieb *owsser betreep*
out aus *ows*
outside draußen *drowssen*

over über *ewber*
over there dort drüben *dort drewben*

P

packet (box) Packung, die *pakoong*
packet (package) Paket, das *pakayt*
pain Schmerz, der *shmerts*
painkillers Schmerztabletten, die *shmertstabletten*
paper Papier, das *papeer*
parasol Sonnenschirm, der *zonnenshirm*
parcel Paket, das *pakayt*
parents Eltern, die (pl) *eltern*
park Park, der *park*
to park parken *parken*
parking fee Parkgebühr, die *paarkgebewr*
passport Reisepass, der *riyzepass*
path Weg, der *vayk*
to pay zahlen, bezahlen *tsaalen betsaalen*
pear Birne, die *birne*
pedestrian zone Fußgängerzone, die *foohssgengertsohne*
penicillin Penizillin, das *penitsileen*
pensioner Rentner/in, der/die *rentner/in*
pepper Pfeffer, der *pfeffer*
per pro *proh*
performance Vorstellung, die *fohrshtelloong*
person Person, die *perzohn*
petrol Benzin, das *bentseen*
petrol station Tankstelle, die *tankshtelle*
photograph Foto, das *fohto*
photographic shop Fotogeschäft, das *fohtogesheft*
piece Stück, das *shtewk*
pizza Pizza, die *pitsa*
plaster Pflaster, das *pflaster*
plastic Plastik, das *plastik*
plate Teller, der *teller*
platform Bahnsteig, der, Gleis, das *baanshtiyg gliys*
to play spielen *shpeelen*
pleasant angenehm *angenaym*
please bitte *bitte*
pleased erfreut *erfroyt*
  I am pleased/glad es freut mich *es froyt mish*
plug Steckdose, die *shtekdohze*
plum cake Zwetschgenkuchen, der *tsvetshgenkoohken*
police Polizei, die *politsiy*
police station Polizeiwache, die *politsiyvake*

policeman Polizist, der *politsist*
politics Politik, die *politeek*
polyester Polyester, das *poliester*
porcelain Porzellan, das *portselaan*
pork Schweinefleisch, das *shviynefliysh*
port Hafen, der *haafen*
portion Portion, die *portsyohn*
post Post, die *post*
postcard Ansichtskarte, die *anzichtskarte*
poster Poster, das *pohster*
pound Pfund, das *pfoont*
pregnant schwanger *shvanger*
prescription Rezept, das *retsept*
pretzel Brezel, die *braytsel*
price Preis, der *priys*
problem Problem, das *problem*
programme Programm, das *programm*
pub Kneipe, die *kniype*
to pull ziehen *tseehen*
pullover Pullover, der *poollohver*
punch (drink) Bowle, die *bohle*
purse Portemonnaie, das *portmonnay*
to push drücken *drewken*
to put stellen *shtellen*
to queue anstellen *anshtellen*
quiet ruhig *roohig*
quite ziemlich *tseemlish*

R

racket Schläger, der *shlayger*
radiator (heating) Heizkörper, der *hiytskerper*
radiator (car engine) Kühler, der *kewler*
rain Regen, der *raygen*
to rain regnen *raygnen*
rain coat Regenjacke, die *raygenyake*
rather ziemlich *tseemlish*
raw roh *roh*
razor blade Rasierklinge, die *razeerklinge*
receipt Quittung, die *kvittoong*
to recommend empfehlen *empfaylen*
red rot *roht*
red wine Rotwein, der *rohtviyn*
to refer (patient) überweisen *ewberviyzen*
registration form Anmeldeformular, das *anmeldeformoolaar*
registration number Autonummer, die *owtonoommer*
remote control Fernbedienung, die *fernbedeenoong*
reservation Reservierung, die *rezerveeroong*
to reserve reservieren *rezerveeren*
restaurant Restaurant, das *restorang*

return ticket Rückfahrkarte, die *rewkfaarkarte*
to ride reiten *riyten*
riding lessons Reitunterricht, der *riytoonterrisht*
right (opposite of left) rechts *reshts*
right (correct) richtig *rishtig*
right of way Vorfahrt, die *fohrfaart*
to ring klingeln *klingeln*
to roast braten *braaten*
roasted gebraten *gebraaten*
room Zimmer, das *tsimmer*
room key Zimmerschlüssel, der *tsimmershlewssel*
room number Zimmernummer, die *tsimmernoommer*
rosé Roséwein, der *rohzayviyn*

S

safe Safe, der *sayf*
to sail segeln *zaygeln*
sailing Segeln, das *zaygeln*
sailing boat Segelboot, das *zaygelboht*
sailing lessons Segelunterricht, der *zaygeloonterrisht*
salad Salat, der *zalaat*
salami Salami, die *zalaamee*
salt Salz, das *zalts*
sandwich belegte Brot, das *belaygte broht*
sauce Soße, die *zohsse*
saucer Untertasse, die *oontertasse*
sauna Sauna, die *zowna*
sausage Wurst, die *voorst*
sautéed gedünstet *gedewnstet*
to say sagen *zaagen*
scarf schal, der *shaal*
schnapps Schnaps, der *shnaps*
sea Meer, das, See, die *mayr zay*
seat Platz, der *plats*
second zweite *tsviyte*
to see sehen *zayen*
self-catering apartment Ferienappartement, das *fayryenappartment*
self-service (café) Selbstbedienung, die *zelpstbedeenoong*
self-service (petrol station) selbsttanken *zelpsttanken*
to send schicken, senden *shiken zenden*
to serve bedienen *bedeenen*
service Bedienung, die *bedeenoong*
service station (motorway) Rastplatz, der *rastplats*
shampoo Shampoo, das *shampooh*
shandy Radler, das *raatler*

shaving cream Rasierschaum, der *razeershowm*

shawl Schal, der *shaal*

she sie *zee*

ship Schiff, das *shiff*

shirt Hemd, das *hemt*

shop Geschäft, das *gesheft*

to shop einkaufen *iynkowfen*

shopping bag Einkaufstasche, die *iynkowfstashe*

shopping centre Einkaufszentrum, das *iynkowfstsentroom*

short kurz *koorts*

show Show, die *shoh*

to show zeigen *tsiygen*

to shower duschen *dooshen*

shower Dusche, die *dooshe*

sick krank *krank*

to be sick sich übergeben *zish ewbergayben*

   I feel sick mir ist übel *meer ist ewbel*

side Seite, die *ziyte*

side dish Beilage, die *biylaage*

side effect Nebenwirkung, die *naybenvirkoong*

sightseeing tour Stadtrundfahrt, die *shtatroontfaart*

to sign unterschreiben *oontershriyben*

silk Seide, die *ziyde*

SIM card SIM-Karte, die *zimkarte,*

single room Einzelzimmer, das *iyntseltsimmer*

single ticket einfache Karte *iynfake kaarte*

to sit sitzen *zitsen*

size Größe, die *grerssee*

to ski Ski fahren *shee faaren*

skis Skier, die *sheeyer*

skiing lessons Skiunterricht, der *sheeoonterrisht*

skirt Rock, der *rok*

slice Scheibe, die *shiybe*

slide Dia, das *deea*

slow langsam *langzaam*

small klein *kliyn*

to smoke rauchen *rowken*

smoked geräuchert *geroyshert*

smoker Raucher, der *rowker*

snack bar Imbiss, der *imbiss*

snail Schnecke, die *shneke*

snowboard Snowboard, das *snohbohrd*

soap Seife, die *ziyfe*

sock Socke, die *zoke*

sole (fish) Scholle, die *sholle*

someone jemand *yaymant*

something etwas *etvas*

soon bald *balt*

I am sorry es tut mir Leid *es tooht meer liyt*

soup Suppe, die *zooppe*

souvenir Reiseandenken, das *riyzeandenken*

sparkling wine Sekt, der *zekt*

to speak sprechen *shpreshen*

specialist Spezialist, der *shpaytsyalist*

speciality of the house Spezialität des Hauses, die *shpaytsyalitayt howzes*

to spell buchstabieren *boohkshtabeeren*

spoon Löffel, der *lerffel*

sports ground Sportanlage, die *shportanlaage*

sports hall Sporthalle, die *shporthalle*

square Platz, der *plats*

spritzer Schorle, die *shorle*

stadium Stadion, das *shtaadyon*

stairs Treppe, die *treppe*

stalls Parkett, das *parkett*

stamp Briefmarke, die *breefmarke*

to stand stehen *shtayen*

start Beginn, der, Anfang, der *beginn anfank*

to start beginnen, anfangen *beginnenanfangen*

starter Vorspeise, die *fohrshpiyze*

station Bahnhof, der *baanhohf*

stay Aufenthalt, der *owfenthalt*

to stay bleiben *bliyben*

to steal stehlen *shtaylen*

steamed gedämpft *gedempft*

steering Lenkung, die *lenkoong*

steering wheel Steuerrad, das *shtoyerraat*

sticker Aufkleber, der *owfklayber*

still noch *nok*

to sting stechen *shteken*

stocking Strumpf, der *shtroompf*

stomach Magen, der *maagen*

stomach ache Magenschmerzen, die (pl) *maagenshmertsen*

storey Stock, der *shtok*

straight ahead geradeaus *geraadeows*

street Straße, die *shtraasse*

subtitle Untertitel, der *oontertitel*

suit (skirt and jacket) Kostüm, das *kostewm*

suit (with trousers) Anzug, der *antsook*

suitcase Koffer, der *koffer*

sun Sonne, die *zonne*

sunglasses Sonnenbrille, die *zonnenbrille*

sunlounger Sonnenliege, die *zonnenleege*
suntan cream Sonnencreme, die *zonnenkraym*
supermarket Supermarkt, der *zoohpermarkt*
supplement Zuschlag, der *tsoohshlaa*
sure, certain sicher *zisher*
to surf surfen *serfen*
surfboard Surfbrett, das *serfbrett*
surfing Surfen, das *serfen*
sweet Süßigkeit, die *zewssigkiyt*
to swim schwimmen *shvimmen*
swimming costume Badeanzug, der *baadeantsook*
swimming hat Badekappe, die *baadekappe*
swimming pool Schwimmbad, das *shvimmbaat*
swimming trunks Badehose, die *baadehohze*

T

to switch off ausschalten *owsshalten*
table Tisch, der *tish*
tablecloth Tischdecke, die *tishdeke*
tablet Tablette, die *tablette*
to take nehmen *naymen*
to talk sprechen *shpreshen*
tankard Bierkrug, der *beerkroohk*
tap Wasserhahn, der *vasserhaan*
taste Geschmack, der *geshmak*
to taste schmecken *shmeken*
to taste (try) probieren *probeeren*
taxi Taxi, das *taksee*
taxi stand Taxistand, der *takseeshtant*
tea Tee, der *tay*
teaspoon Teelöffel, der *taylerffel*
telephone Telefon, das *telefohn*
to telephone telefonieren *telefoneeren*
telephone card Telefonkarte, die *telefohnkarte*
television Fernseher, der *fernzayer*
tennis Tennis, das *tennis*
  tennis court Tennisplatz, der *tennisplats*
  tennis match Tennisspiel, das *tennisshpeel*
  tennis racket Tennisschläger, der *tennisshlayger*
terrace Terrasse, die *terrasse*
to thank danken *danken*
thank you danke *danke*
that dass *dass*
the der, die das *der, dee, das*
theatre Theater, das *tayaater*
them sie, (to them) ihnen *zee, eenen*
there da, dort *daa, dort*

there is/are es gibt *es geept*
they sie *zee*
thigh Oberschenkel, der *ohbershenkel*
this dies *dees*
throat Hals, der *hals*
ticket Fahrkarte, die, Ticket, das, (admission) Eintrittskarte, die *faarkarte tiket iyntrittskarte*
ticket office Schalter, der *shalter*
tie Krawatte, die *kravatte*
tights Strumpfhose, die *shtroompfhohze*
till Kasse, die *kasse*
time Zeit, die *tsiyt*
what time is it? wie spät ist es? *vee shpayt ist es*
timetable Fahrplan, der *faarplaan*
tin Dose, die *dohze*
tip Trinkgeld, das *trinkgelt*
tissue Taschentuch, das *tashentoohk*
to zu *tsooh*
toe Zeh, der *tsay*
together zusammen *tsoozammen*
toilet Toilette, die *toalette*
toilet paper Toilettenpapier, das *toalettenpapeer*
tomato Tomate, die *tomaate*
tomorrow morgen *morgen*
too zu *tsooh*
tools Werkzeug, das *vayrktsoyk*
tooth Zahn, der *tsaan*
toothache Zahnschmerzen, die (pl) *tsaanshmertsen*
toothbrush Zahnbürste, die *tsaanbewrste*
toothpaste Zahnpasta, die *tsaanpasta*
toothpick Zahnstocher, der *tsaanshtoker*
tourist information Touristeninformation, die *tooristeninformatsyohn*
tourist office Fremdenverkehrsbüro, das *fremdenferkayrsbewro*
towel Handtuch, das *hanttoohk*
towelling Frottee, das *frottay*
town Stadt, die *shtat*
town hall Rathaus, das *raathows*
tracksuit Trainingsanzug, der *trayningsantsook*
train Zug, der *tsoohk*
train station Bahnhof, der *baanhohf*
tram Straßenbahn, die *shtraassenbaahn*
to transfer (money) überweisen *ewberviyzen*
to travel reisen *riyzen*
travel guide Reiseführer, der *riyzefewrer*

traveller's cheque Reisescheck, der
  riyzeshek
tray Tablett, das *tablett*
tree Baum, der *bowm*
trip Fahrt, die *faart*
to try on anprobieren *anprobeeren*
trousers Hose, die *hohze*
t-shirt T-Shirt, das *teeshirt*
tyre Reifen, der *riyfen*

U

umbrella Regenschirm, der
  raygenshirm
under unter *oonter*
underdone roh *roh*
underground (tube) U-Bahn, die
  oohbaan
to understand verstehen *fershtayen*
unfortunately leider *liyder*
university Universität, die
  ooniverzitayt
unleaded bleifrei *bliyfriy*
until bis *bis*
upstairs oben *ohben*
urgent dringend *dringent*
to use benutzen *benootsen*

V

value-added tax (VAT)
  Mehrwertsteuer, die
  mayrvayrtshtoyer
vegetable Gemüse, das *gemewze*
vegetarian Vegetarier/in, der/die,
  vegetarisch *vegetaaryer/in*
  vegetaarish
very sehr *zayr*
vinegar Essig, der *essig*
volleyball Volleyball, der *vollayball*

W

to wait for warten auf *varten owf*
waiter Ober, der, Kellner, der *ohber*
  kellner
waiting room Wartesaal, der
  vartezaal
waitress Kellnerin, die, Bedienung,
  die *kellnerin bedeenoong*
to wake wecken *veken*
to walk laufen *lowfen*
walking stick Wanderstock, der
  vandershtok
walkman Walkman, der *vokmen*
wallet Brieftasche, die *breeftashe*
warm warm *vaarm*
to wash waschen *vashen*
waste bin Mülleimer, der *mewlliymer*
watch Uhr, die *oohr*
water Wasser, das *vasser*

waterskis Wasserskier, die
  vassersheer
to water-ski Wasserski fahren
  vassershee faaren
waterskiing Wasserski, das
  vassershee
welcome (herzlich) willkommen
  (hertslish) villkommen
you're welcome keine Ursache, bitte
  kiyne oohrzake, bitte
what was *vas*
wheel Rad, das *raat*
when wann *vann*
where wo *voh*
where ... from woher *vohher*
where ... to wohin *vohhin*
which welche *velshe*
white weiß *viyss*
white wine Weißwein, der *viyssviyn*
wholemeal bread Vollkornbrot, das
  follkornbroht
why warum *varoom*
wind Wind, der *vint*
window Fenster, das *fenster*
windscreen Windschutzscheibe, die
  vintshootsshiybe
windscreen wiper Scheibenwischer,
  der *shiybenvisher*
to windsurf windsurfen *vintserfen*
windsurfing Windsurfen, das
  vintserfen
wine Wein, der *viyn*
with mit *mit*
without ohne *ohne*
woman Frau, die *frow*
wool Wolle, die *volle*
woollen hat Mütze, die *mewtse*
to work (function) funktionieren
  foonktsyoneeren
to write schreiben *shriyben*
to write down aufschreiben
  owfshriyben

Y

yellow gelb *gelp*
yes ja *yaa*
yesterday gestern *gestern*
yet noch *nok*
yoghurt Joghurt, der *yohgoort*
you Sie (formal), du (informal) *zee,*
  dooh
youth hostel Jugendherberge, die
  yoohgentherbayrge

Z

zero null *nooll*

A

Abend, der evening
Abendessen, das   evening meal
abends in the evening
aber but
abfahren to depart
Abfahrt, die departure, exit off
  motorway
Abfahrtslauf, der downhill skiing
abgeben to hand in
Abzweigung, die turn off
Adresse, die address
Aktenkoffer, der briefcase
Alkohol, der alcohol
alkoholfrei non-alcoholic
alkoholisch alcoholic
alle everyone
Allergie, die allergy
allergisch allergic
alles everything
Altstadt, die old town
Anfang, der start, beginning
anfangen to start, to begin
angenehm pleasant
Angorawolle, die angora
Ankunft, die arrival
Anmeldeformular, das registration form
anprobieren to try on
Ansichtskarte, die postcard
sich anstellen to queue
Anzug, der suit (with trousers)
Apfel, der apple
Apotheke, die chemist's
Arm, der arm
Arzt, der/Ärztin, die doctor
Aschenbecher, der ash tray
auch also
auf on
Aufenthalt, der stay
Auffahrt, die approach road
Aufkleber, der sticker
Aufschnitt, der cold meat
aufschreiben to write down
aufstehen to get up
Auge, das eye
aus out, from
ausfüllen to fill out
Ausgang, der exit
ausgezeichnet excellent
Auskunft, die information
aussehen to look like
außer apart from
außer Betrieb out of order
aussteigen to get off, out
Ausstellung, die exhibition
Ausweis, der identity/membership card
Auto, das car

Autobahn, die motorway
Autokennzeichen, das registration
  number
Autowerkstatt, die garage

B

Babystuhl, der high chair
Bäckerei, die bakery
Bad, das bath
Badeanzug, der swimming costume
Badehose, die swimming trunks
Badekappe, die swimming hat
Badetuch, das beach towel
Badezimmer, das bathroom
Bahnhof, der train station
Bahnsteig, der platform
bald soon
Balkon, der balcony
Ball, der ball
Banane, die banana
Bank, die bank, bench
bar cash
Bar, die bar
Batterie, die battery
Bauernbrot, das bread made from sour
  dough
Baum, der tree
Baumwolle, die cotton
Becher, der cup, beaker
bedeuten to mean
bedienen to serve
Bedienung, die service, waiter/ waitress
bei near
Beilage, die side dish
Bein, das leg
beißen to bite
Bekleidungsgeschäft, das clothes' shop
bekommen to get, receive
belegtes Brot (das) sandwich
benutzen to use
Benzin, das petrol
Berg, der hill, mountain
Bergsteigen, das mountaineering
Beruf, der job, occupation
besser better
Besteck, das cutlery
bestellen to order
Bett, das bed
Bettwäsche, die sheets, bed linen
bezahlen to pay
Bier, das beer
Biergarten, der beer garden
Bierkrug, der tankard
Bikini, der bikini
billig cheap
Birne, die pear, light bulb
bis until, as far as
bisschen, ein bisschen a bit, a little (of)

bitte please, you're welcome
blau blue
bleiben to stay, remain
bleifrei unleaded
Bluse, die blouse
Boot, das boat
Bowle, die punch
braten to roast, bake
brauchen to need
braun brown
brechen to break
Bremse, die brake (on a vehicle)
Brezel, die pretzel
Brief, der letter
Briefmarke, die stamp
Briefpapier, das notepaper
Brieftasche, die wallet
Brille, die glasses
Brot, das bread
Brötchen, das bread roll
Brücke, die bridge
Brust, die chest
Buch, das book
Buchladen, der bookshop
buchstabieren to spell
Bügeleisen, das iron
bügeln to iron
Bus, der bus
Bushaltestelle, die bus stop
Butter, die butter

C

Café, das café
Campingplatz, der camping site
CD, die CD
Cola, die cola
Creme, die cream

D

da there
Dame, die lady
Damenabteilung, die ladies'
    department
danke thank you
danken to thank
das the, that
dass that
Dia, das slide
dies this
Digitalkamera, die digital camera
Disko, die disco
Doppelzimmer, das double room
dort there
dort drüben over there
Dose, die tin, can
draußen outside
dringend urgent
Drogerie, die drug store (not
    pharmacy)

drücken to push, press
du you (informal)
dürfen to be allowed, may
Dusche, die shower
duschen to shower

E

Ecke, die corner
Edamer, der Edam cheese
Ei, das egg
Einbahnstraße, die one way street
einfach easy
einfach single (ticket)
Eingang, der entrance
einkaufen to buy, shop
Einkaufstasche, die shopping bag
Einkaufszentrum, das shopping
    centre
einlösen (Geld) to exchange money
einmal once
Eintritt, der entry, admission
Eintrittskarte, die ticket (of
    admission)
Einzelzimmer, das single room
Eis, das ice-cream
Eisdiele, die ice-cream parlour
Ellbogen, der elbow
Eltern, die (pl) parents
empfehlen to recommend
Ende, das end
enthalten to contain
Entschuldigung excuse me!
entwickeln to develop
er he
Erdgeschoss, das ground floor
Erkältung, die cold
Ermäßigung, die concession
erste first
Erwachsene(r), der/die adult
es it
Espresso, der espresso
essen to eat
Essen, das food
Essig, der vinegar
etwas something
Europäische
    Krankenversicherungskarte, die
    European Health Insurance Card, EHIC

F

fahren to drive, go
Fahrer, der driver
Fahrkarte, die ticket
Fahrplan, der timetable
Fahrrad, das bicycle
Fahrradweg, der cycle path
Fahrstuhl, der lift
Fahrt, die trip, journey
Familie, die family

fangen to catch
fantastisch fantastic
Farbe, die colour
Fehler, der mistake
Ferien, die (pl) holidays
Ferienappartement, das self-catering
   apartment
Fernbedienung, die remote control
Fernsehen, das television
Fernseher, der television
fertig finished, ready
Feuerwehr, die fire brigade
Feuerwerk, das fireworks
Feuerzeug, das (cigarette) lighter
Fieber, das fever
Film, der film, camera film
finden to find
Finger, der finger
Fisch, der fish
Fitnessraum, der gym
Flasche, die bottle
Fleisch, das meat
Fleischer, der butcher
Flohmarkt, der flea market
Flunder, die flounder
Flughafen, der airport
Flugzeug, das aeroplane
Fondue, das fondue
Formular, das form
Foto, das photograph, print
Fotogeschäft, das photographic shop
Frankfurter Kranz, der Frankfurt coffee
   gâteau
Frau, die woman, Mrs
frei free
Fremdenverkehrsbüro, das tourist office
sich freuen to be glad/pleased
   es freut mich dass I'm glad/pleased
   that
   ich freue mich auf I'm looking forward
   to
   ich freue mich über I'm glad/pleased
   about
froh happy
Frottee, das towelling
Frühstück, das breakfast
fühlen to feel
Führerschein, der driving licence
Führung, die guided tour
Fundbüro, das lost property office
funktionieren to work, function
Fuß, der foot
Fußball, der football
Fußballspiel, das football match
Fußgängerzone, die pedestrian zone
Fußknöchel, der ankle

G

Gabel, die fork
Galerie, die gallery
Garderobe, die cloakroom
Garten, der garden
Gaspedal, das accelerator
Gästezimmer, das guestroom
Gasthaus, das guesthouse, inn
Gasthof, der guesthouse, inn
geben to give
   es gibt there is, there are
gebraten fried, roasted
gebrochen broken
Gebühr, die charge, fee
gedämpft steamed
gedünstet sautéed
gefallen: es gefällt mir I like it
gefüllt filled, stuffed
gegen against
gegenüber opposite
gegrillt grilled
Geländelauf, der cross-country run
gelb yellow
Geld, das money
Geldautomat, der cash machine
gemischt mixed
Gemüse, das vegetable
Genick, das neck
Gepäck, das luggage
geradeaus straight ahead
geräuchert smoked
Gericht, das meal, dish/court
Gerstenbier, das beer made from barley
Geschäft, das business, shop
Geschäftsmann/frau, der/die business
   man/woman
Geschäftsreise, die business trip
Geschmack, der taste, flavour
gestern yesterday
Getränk, das drink
Glas, das glass
glauben to believe
gleich immediately
Gleis, das platform
Glück, das luck
glücklich happy
Glühbirne, die light bulb
Golf, das golf
Golfplatz, der golf course
Golfschläger, der golf club
Gramm, das gram
groß big
Größe, die size
grün green
Gurke, die cucumber
Gürtel, der belt
gut good

H

Haar, das hair
Haartrockner, der hairdryer
haben to have
Hafen, der harbour
halb half
Halbpension, die half-board
Hälfte, die half
hallo hello
Hals, der throat, neck
Halsschmerzen, die (pl) sore throat
halten to hold, keep
Hand, die hand
Handy, das mobile phone
Handschuh, der glove
Handtasche, die handbag
Handtuch, das towel
Hauptbahnhof, der main station
Hauptgericht, das main course
Hauptspeise, die main course
Haus, das house
hausgemacht homemade
Haushaltsabteilung, die household
  department
heiß hot
heißen to be called
Heizung, die heating
helfen help
Hemd, das shirt
Herr, der Mann, Mr
Herrenabteilung, die men's
  department
Herz, das heart
Herzanfall, der heart attack
Herzinfarkt, der heart attack
Heuriger, der young wine
Heuschnupfen der hayfever
hier here
Hilfe, die help
sich hinlegen to lie down
Hin und zurück return ticket
hinter behind
hoch high
Hochglanz, der glossy
holen to get, fetch
Hörnchen, das type of croissant
Hose, die trousers
Hotel, das hotel
Hüfte, die hip
Hund, der dog
Husten, der cough
husten to cough
Hustensaft, der cough medicine
Hut, der hat

I

ich I
Imbiss, der snack bar

in in
Infektion, die infection
Information, die information
inklusiv inclusive
Inline-Skates, die (pl) inline-skates
Innenstadt, die city centre
interessant interesting
sich interessieren für to be interested
  in
international international
Internetcafé, das internet café
Internetzugang, der internet access

J

ja yes
Jacke, die jacket
Jackett, das jacket
Jeans, die (pl) jeans
jemand someone
Joghurt, der yoghurt
Jugendherberge, die youth hostel
Juwelier jeweller's

K

Kaffee, der coffee
kalt cold
Kännchen, das small pot
Karaffe, die carafe, jug
Käse, der cheese
Kasse, die till
Kassette, die cassette case, box
Katalog, der catalogue
Kathedrale, die cathedral
Katze, die cat
kaufen to buy
Kaufhaus, das department store
Kellner/in, der/die waiter/waitress
Ketchup, der/das ketchup
Kette, die chain, necklace
Kilo, das kilo
Kilometer, der kilometre
Kind, das child
Kinderbett, das children's bed
Kinn, das chin
Kino, das cinema
Kiosk, der kiosk
Kirche, die church
Kirsche, die cherry
Kiwi, die kiwi fruit
Klasse, die class
  erste/zweite Klasse first/second
  class
Kleid, das dress
klein small, little
Kleingeld, das change
Klimaanlage, die air-conditioning
klingen to sound
klingeln to ring
Kneipe, die pub

Knie, das knee
Knochen, der bone
koffeinfreier Kaffee, der decaffeinated coffee
Koffer, der suitcase
kommen to come
Kommission, die commission
Kompott, das stewed fruit
Konditorei, die cake shop, café
Konferenzraum, der conference room
Konzert, das concert
Kopf, der head
Kopfschmerzen, die (pl) headache
Kopfschmerztabletten, die headache tablets
Korb, der basket
kosten to cost
Kostüm, das suit (skirt and jacket)
Krankenhaus, das hospital
Krankenschein, der health insurance certificate/policy
Krankenwagen, der ambulance
Krawatte, die tie
Kreditkarte, die credit card
Kreuzung, die crossing
Kuchen, der cake
Kuckucksuhr, die cuckoo clock
Kugelschreiber, der ballpoint pen
Kuhglocke, die cowbell
Kühler, der radiator
Kultur, die culture
kulturell cultural
Kunst, die art
Kupplung, die clutch
Kurs, der exchange rate
kurz short

L

lang long
langsam slow, slowly
Laptop, der laptop
lassen to let, leave
laufen to walk, run
Leber, die liver
Lebkuchen, der gingerbread
Leder, das leather
es tut mir Leid I am sorry
leider unfortunately
leihen to hire
Lenkung, die steering
Licht, das light
liegen to lie
Liegestuhl, der deckchair
Limonade, die lemonade
links left
Liter, der/das litre
Löffel, der spoon
Luft, die air

Luftpost, die airmail
Lycra, das lycra

M

machen to make, do
Magen, der stomach
Magenschmerzen, die (pl) stomach ache
Mantel, der coat
Margarine, die margarine
Markt, der market
Marktplatz, der market place/square
Marzipantorte, die marzipan gâteau
matt matt
Medikament, das medicine
Medizin, die medicine
Meer, das sea
mehr more
Mehrwertsteuer, die value-added tax (VAT)
Melone, die melon
Messe, die exhibition, fair
Messer, das knife
Metzger, der butcher
mieten to hire
Milch, die milk
Milchkaffee, der white coffee
Mineralwasser, das mineral water
mit with
Mittagessen, das lunch
mittags lunch time
mögen to like
Mokka, der strong, black coffee
Moment, der moment
morgen tomorrow
Morgen, der morning
morgens in the morning
Moselwein, der wine from the Moselle
Motor, der engine
Mountainbike, das mountain bike
Mountainbike fahren to go mountain biking
MP3-Player mp3 player
Mülleimer, der waste bin
Mund, der mouth
Muschel, die mussel
Museum, das museum
Musical, das musical
müssen to have to, must
Mütze, die woollen hat

N

nach after, towards
Nachmittag, der afternoon
nachmittags in the afternoon
nächste next
Nachtisch, der dessert
nacht, die night
  nachts at night

Nachtklub, der night club
Nagel, der nail
nah near
Nähe, die, in der Nähe near
Name, der name
natürlich of course
neben next to
Nebenwirkung, die side effect
nehmen to take
nein no
neu new
nicht not
Nichtraucher, der non-smoker
nichts nothing
niedrig low
niemand no one
Niere, die kidney
noch yet, still
Notausgang, der emergency exit
null nought, zero
Nummer, die number
nummeriert numbered
nur only
Nusstorte, die cream gâteau with nuts
Nylon, das nylon

O

oben upstairs
Ober, der waiter
Oberschenkel, der thigh
Obst, das fruit
Obstkuchen, der fruit flan
Öffnungszeit, die opening hours
oft often
ohne without
Ohr, das ear
Öl, das oil
Oper, die opera
operieren to operate
Optiker, der optician's
Orange orange (fruit)
orange orange (colour)
Orangensaft, der orange juice
alles in Ordnung? everything okay?

P

Packung, die packet
Paket, das packet
Panne, die to break down
eine Panne haben to have a puncture
Papier, das paper
Papiere, die (pl) ID papers
Park, der park
parken to park
Parkett, das stalls
Parkgebühr, die charge for parking
Parkplatz, der car park
passen to fit, suit, be convenient

passieren to happen, occur
Pause, die break
Penizillin, das penicillin
Pension, die boarding house
Person, die person
Pfeffer, der pepper
Pflaster, das plaster
Pfund, das pound
Pilsner, das Pils, strong lager
Pizza, die pizza
Plastik, das plastic
Platz, der square
Platz, der place, seat
Platz im Schlafwagen, der couchette
Plombe, die filling
Politik, die politics
Polizei, die police
Polizeiwache, die police station
Polizist, der policeman
Polyester, das polyester
Pommes frites, die (pl) chips
Portemonnaie, das purse
Portion, die portion
Porzellan, das porcelain
Post, die post
Poster, das poster
Postkarte, die post card
Preis, der price
pro per
probieren to taste, try
Problem, das problem
Programm, das programme
Pullover, der pullover
Puppe, die doll

Q

Quittung, die receipt

R

Rad, das wheel, bike
Radler, das shandy
Rasierklinge, die razor blade
Rasierschaum, der shaving cream
Rastplatz, der (motorway) service station
Rathaus, das town hall
rauchen to smoke
Raucher, der smoker
Rechnung, die bill
rechts right
Regen, der rain
Regenjacke, die raincoat
Regenschirm, der umbrella
regnen to rain
Reifen, der tyre
Reise, die trip, journey
Reiseandenken, das souvenir
Reiseführer, der travel guide
reisen to travel

Reisepass, der passport
Reisescheck, der traveller's cheque
reiten to ride
Reitunterricht, der riding lessons
Rentner/in, der/die pensioner
reservieren to reserve
Reservierung, die reservation
Restaurant, das restaurant
Rezept, das prescription
Rheinwein, der wine from the Rhineland
richtig right, correct
Rock, der skirt
roh raw, underdone
Rollo, das blind
Roséwein, der rosé
rot red
Rotwein, der red wine
Rücken, der back
Rückenschmerzen, die (pl) backache
Rückfahrkarte, die return ticket
Ruhe, die silence, calm, rest
ruhig quiet, still, calm

S

Sachertorte, die chocolate cake
Sackgasse, die cul-de-sac
Safe, der safe
Saft, der juice
sagen to say
Sahne, die cream
Salami, die salami
Salat, der salad
Salz, das salt
Sauna, die sauna
Schal, der scarf, shawl
Schale, die dessert bowl
Schalter, der counter, ticket office
schauen to look
Scheibe, die slice
Scheibe, die window pane
Scheibenwischer, der windscreen wiper
schicken to send
Schiff, das ship
Schinken, der ham
Schinkenwurst, die ham sausage
Schlafwagen, der couchette
Schläger, der racket
schlimm bad
Schloss, das castle
Schloss, das lock
Schlüssel, der key
schmecken to taste
Schmerz, der pain
Schmerztablette, die pain killer
Schmuck, der jewellery
Schmuckgeschäft, das jeweller's
Schnaps, der schnapps
Schnecke, die snail

schneiden to cut
Schokolade, die chocolate
Schokoladentorte, die chocolate gâteau
Scholle, die sole
schön beautiful
Schorle, die spritzer
Schrank, der cupboard, locker
schreiben to write
Schreibwarenladen, der stationer's
Schurwolle, die pure wool
schwanger pregnant
schwarz black
Schwarzbrot, das dark bread
Schwarzwälder Schinken, der type of
   smoked ham
Schweinefleisch, das pork
schwierig difficult, hard
Schwimmbad, das swimming pool
schwimmen to swim
See, der lake
See, die sea
Segelboot, das sailing boat
segeln to sail
Segeln, das sailing
Segelunterricht, der sailing lessons
sehen to see
sehr very
Seide, die silk
Seife, die soap
sein to be
Seite, die side
Sekt, der sparkling wine, champagne
Selbstbedienung, die self-service (in a
   restaurant, café)
selbsttanken self-service (petrol
   station)
selbstverständlich of course
senden to send
Senf, der mustard
Serviette, die napkin
Shampoo, das shampoo
Show, die show
sicher sure, certain
sie she, her, they, them
Sie you (formal)
SIM-Karte, die SIM card
sitzen to sit
Skiunterricht, der skiing lessons
Snowboard, das snowboard
Socke, die sock
sofort immediately
Sonne, die sun
Sonnenbrille, die sunglasses
Sonnencreme, die suntan cream
Sonnenliege, die sunlounger
Sonnenschirm, der parasol
sonst noch etwas anything else

Sorte, die kind, variety, flavour (ice cream)
Soße, die sauce
Souvenir, das souvenir
spät late
wie spät ist es? what's the time?
Speicherkarte, die memory card
Speisekarte, die menu
Speisesaal, der dining-room
Spezialist, der specialist
Spezialität des Hauses, die speciality of the house
Spiegel, der mirror
Spiel, das game, match
spielen to play
Sportanlage, die sports ground
Sporthalle, die sports hall
sprechen to speak, talk
Stadion, das stadium
Stadt, die town, city
Stadtplan, der map
Stadtrundfahrt, die sightseeing tour
stechen prick, sting, bite, stab
Steckdose, die plug
stehen to stand
stehlen to steal
steigen climb
stellen to put
Stellplatz, der site
Steuerrad, das steering wheel
Stiefel, der boot
Stock, der floor, storey
Strand, der beach
Straße, die street
Straßenbahn, die tram
Strumpf, der stocking
Strumpfhose, die tights
Stück, das piece
Stuhl, der chair
Stunde, die hour, lesson
suchen to look for
Supermarkt, der supermarket
Suppe, die soup
Surfbrett, das surfboard
surfen to surf
Surfen, das surfing
Süßigkeit, die sweet

T

T-Shirt, das T-Shirt
Tablett, das tray
Tablette, die tablet
Tag, der day
Tagesgericht, das dish of the day
Tageskarte, die daily travel card
täglich daily
Tankstelle, die petrol station
Tasche, die bag

Taschentuch, das tissue
Tasse, die cup
tauschen to exchange, change
Taxi, das taxi
Taxistand, der taxi stand
Tee, der tea
Teelöffel, der teaspoon
Teewurst, die smoked sausage spread
Telefon, das telephone
telefonieren to telephone
Telefonkarte, die telephone card
Teller, der plate
Tennis, das tennis
Tennisplatz, der tennis court
Tennisschläger, der tennis racket
Tennisspiel, das tennis match
Terrasse, die terrace
teuer expensive
Theater, das theatre
Ticket, das ticket
Tisch, der table
Tischdecke, die tablecloth
Toilette, die toilet
Toilettenpapier, das toilet paper
Tomate, die tomato
Torte, die gâteau
Touristeninformation, die tourist information
Trainingsanzug, der tracksuit
Traube, die grape
Traubensaft, der grape juice
Treppe, die staircase, stairs
trinken to drink
Trinkgeld, das tip
Tropfen, der drop
tschüss bye
tun to do, make

U

U-Bahn, die underground, tube
Übelkeit, die sickness and nausea
über over
überfallen to attack, mug, assault
überweisen to transfer, refer
Uhr, die watch, clock
um at, around
Umkleidekabine, die changing room/cubicle
Umleitung, die diversion
umsteigen to change (trains)
und and
Unfall, der accident
Unfallstation, die casualty department
ungefähr about
Universität, die university
unten downstairs
unter under
Untergeschoss, das basement

unterschreiben to sign
untersuchen to examine, investigate
Untertasse, die saucer
Untertitel, der subtitle
Urlaub, der holiday

V

Vegetarier/in, der/die vegetarian
vegetarisch vegetarian
Veranstaltungskalender, der entertainment guide
Verbandskasten, der first-aid box
verbrannt burnt
Verbrennung, die burn
Verdauungsbeschwerde, die indigestion
Versicherung, die insurance
verlassen to leave, depart, check out
verletzt hurt, injured
verlieren to lose
Versicherungsnummer, die insurance number
verstehen to understand
viel much, a lot
Volleyball, der volley ball
Vollkornbrot, das wholemeal bread
Vollpension, die full board
voll tanken to fill up (with petrol)
von from
vor in front of, before
Vorfahrt, die right of way, priority
Vorspeise, die starter
vorstellen to introduce
Vorstellung, die performance

W

wachsen to grow
wählen to choose, dial
Walkman, der walkman
wandern to go hiking
Wanderstock, der walking stick
wann when
warm warm
warten auf to wait for
Wartesaal, der waiting room
warum why
was what
waschen to wash
Waschsalon, der launderette
Waschstraße, die car-wash
Wasser, das water
Wasserhahn, der tap
Wasserski, der water-ski
Wasserski, das water-skiing
Wechselgeld, das change
wecken to wake
Wecker, der alarm clock
Weg, der path
Wegwerfkamera, die disposable camera
weh tun, es tut mir weh it hurts

Wein, der wine
weiß white
Weißkohl, der cabbage
Weißwein, der white wine
weit far
weitergehen to continue
Weizenbier, das light beer, brewed with wheat
welche which
wenig little, not much
werden to become
Werkzeug, das tools
wie how
wieder again
Wiedersehen, auf Wiedersehen goodbye
willkommen, herzlich willkommen welcome
Wind, der wind
Windschutzscheibe, die windscreen
windsurfen to windsurf
Windsurfen, das windsurfing
wissen to know
wo where
woher where … from
wohin where … to
wohnen to live
Wohnwagen, der caravan
Wolle, die wool
Wurst, die sausage

Z

zählen to count
zahlen to pay
Zahn, der tooth
Zahnbürste, die toothbrush
Zahnpasta, die toothpaste
Zahnschmerzen, die (pl) toothache
Zahnstocher, der toothpick
Zeh, der toe
zeigen to show
Zeit, die time
Zeitschrift, die magazine
Zeitschriftenhändler, der newsagent's
Zeitung, die newspaper
Zentrum, das centre
ziehen to pull
ziemlich quite, rather, fairly
Zigarette, die cigarette
Zimmer, das room
Zimmernummer, die room number
Zimmerschlüssel, der room key
Zitrone, die lemon
zu to, too
zu Ende finished, over
Zug, der train
zusammen together
Zuschlag, der supplement